Imagine . . .
The greatest day of your life.
Imagine that you're at the set in Van Nuys, California, where the smash TV series Beverly Hills, 90210 *is filmed.*
Imagine that you're a lucky reporter who's been invited to spend the day talking to the stars, watching them work, hanging with them when they have a few minutes free.
Imagine that Jason Priestley has just taken off from the set for a few moments of fresh air before rehearsals start again.
What would it be like to follow him outside . . . ?

LUKE MANIA! JASON FEVER!

JEFF ROVIN

FANTAIL

FANTAIL BOOKS

Published by the Penguin Group
Penguin Books Ltd, 27 Wrights Lane, London W8 5TZ, England
Penguin Books USA Inc., 375 Hudson Street, New York, New York 10014, USA
Penguin Books Australia Ltd, Ringwood, Victoria, Australia
Penguin Books Canada Ltd, 10 Alcorn Avenue, Toronto, Ontario, Canada M4V 3B2
Penguin Books (NZ) Ltd, 182–190 Wairau Road, Auckland 10, New Zealand

Penguin Books Ltd, Registered Offices: Harmondsworth, Middlesex, England

First published in the USA by Jove Books 1991
Published in Fantail Books 1992
1 3 5 7 9 10 8 6 4 2

Acknowledgments

Many reporters and researchers, publicists and actors, personal managers and agents contributed their talents to this work. The "day" covered in this book was actually several days, and it was drawn from the experiences of a number of different interviewers. The stars' comments have been fleshed out using interviews from other sources. However, all of the quotes attributed to the actors were actually made by the actors.

The author's intent has been to recreate what just one single interviewer (you, the reader!) would experience if you were able to visit the set of *Beverly Hills, 90210*.

Hope you enjoy your trip there!

Chapter 1

It's a *really* nutty question, and you half-expect Jason Priestley to answer it with a characteristic joke. Either that or pop you in the nose.

But he doesn't. He takes your question very, very seriously.

You ask, Is there any part of his body that Jason wishes were *different*?

Now, if you're a fan of the TV mega-star, you're probably scratching your head and wondering, What could Jason wish were different? How can you improve on perfection?

And what kind of melonhead would even *ask* such a dumb question?

Well . . . you ask it for the same reason you ask *any* question. Because you're curious.

You're standing just a few yards away from the busy warehouse that serves as a soundstage where the smash TV series *Beverly Hills, 90210* is filmed. There was a break in rehearsals, and when Luke Perry hurried one way and Jason Priestley went another, you followed Jason out here.

You're here to interview the two stars, but you wanted to start by asking Jason something *different*, something he's probably never been asked before. And that's what you came up with.

Now you watch him closely. His mouth forms a boyish little smile, like he's hiding something. He takes a sip of black coffee from a styrofoam cup, slips off the hexagonal sunglasses he's rarely without, hooks them over the pocket of his shirt, and fixes those magical blue-green eyes on you.

"Guess," he says.

You look at the face that's got the best features of James Spader and Tom Cruise rolled into one stunning package (and is more glorious than those two poor, less fortunate dudes). You try hard to guess.

"Uh . . . is it a mole or something that can't be seen?"

He shakes his head, and you continue to study the stunning, twenty-two-year-old super-celebrity standing in front of you.

Now that you've created a mystery, you've only got five minutes to solve it, to be the first to learn a secret about one of the country's two newest and greatest heartthrobs. If you fail, it'll be *hours* before lunchtime, which is when you'll get to sit down and talk to him at length.

You wonder—

Is the adorable Jason, a guy who loves practical jokes, pulling your leg?

It's possible. One of the crew members you were talking to earlier said that he always gives people a little *smile* when he kids them. And right now, he's smiling.

But still, you can't be sure he's joking, so you look him over.

His moderately long, sandy brown hair looks almost blond in the bright Southern California sun, and a long strand has fallen across his forehead, over his left eye. You notice that his hair is fine and straight—could he possibly wish that it were thicker? Wavier? Curlier?

No way! It's perfection just the way it is.

You check out the eyebrows, which are thick and straight. When he smiles, they arch in the center, framing his eyes. Could he wish that they were thinner? That they didn't look *quite* so brooding when he's

10

lost in thought or concentrating on learning his lines?

Uh-uh. That look is *intense*. Later, when you talk in his trailer, you realize that those eyebrows are like two powerful magnets, drawing you in.

The eyes? Could he wish his eyes were a different shape?

That's the most unlikely notion of all! Not even Jason on his *most* critical day could find anything wrong with them. They've been described as "puppy dog eyes," but the dog that comes to mind is a *hot dog*—a crack fighter pilot. The eyes are alert, deep, and intelligent. They're able to size up and grasp a situation in an instant. When they're not examining whatever is going on outside the man, they're showing you what's going on inside, clear windows into the soul of the sensitive young actor.

His nose?

Not! It's straight and strong and perfect.

You tell yourself that maybe you should give up— you're *never* going to find anything but Grade A material on this guy!

Chapter 2

Jason untangles the gold ID bracelet he wears on his left wrist, then checks the watch on his right.

"So?" he urges. "What do you think?"

"I'm not sure," you tell him, wishing you'd asked some ordinary question like *What's your favorite movie?*

You study the square line of his jaw, which ends in a mature, manly chin. There are the hints of dimples in his cheeks, and *no one* would mind having those.

What about the mouth?

The ends turn down, giving them a pouty look, as though Jason's carrying the weight of the world on his shoulders. But there's an incredible *sensuousness* to those lips, and when he smiles, the weight seems to vanish. Can't find a thing wrong with those lips.

Jason's smile broadens and he sips more coffee. You know what that big smile means: he knows he's *got* you. Like Rapunzel, you're not going to guess his secret in the few minutes that are left. Still, instead of giving up, you hurry up.

He's wearing tight, dark jeans and a loose-fitting green polo shirt, the short sleeves rolled up to the shoulders. Though he's no Arnold Schwarzenegger, he's no wimp either. He's got a slender build, but he moves with amazing grace, even off-camera. You're not surprised when you learn that he studied dance when he was a teenager.

His neck is long and thin, and his hands are delicate but masculine. He stands five feet eight inches tall—not a giant, but Jason's well proportioned and wiry. And as you find out from talking with him later, he's never believed that a person's size is measured by their height. It's the size of what's *inside* that makes a person big or small—the size of their heart and their ability to give.

Which brings you back to your own dumb question: What could he *possibly* wish to change?

He hooks the empty cup into a garbage barrel—a three-pointer, from this distance—and looks toward the soundstage, where director Jeff Melman is talking to an assistant in the doorway. Then Jason says, "I've got to get back to work."

"But wait!" you cry.

"Later," he says, dude-cool as he steps from the brilliant daylight into the dark soundstage.

You follow him in, making your way around lights and microphones, stepping over cables thick as garden hoses. Security people and technicians are standing around, chatting about this and that as they eat donuts that are stacked in boxes on a table just inside the door. You wonder, as you pass, how they can be so *casual* about working here . . . *here*, where Jason Priestley and Luke Perry rule!

You know that *you'd* have given away your collection of New Kids tapes, and probably your little brother, too, just to be one of them, just to work with the reigning princes of the airwaves.

The soundstage through which you're making your way is larger than a football field and bigger than an airplane hangar. The rooms that are so familiar from the TV show are here, and they look—*weird* in person.

For one thing, they're *very* brightly lit. Since a lot of light gets lost when pictures are transmitted to your

13

television set, the sets have to be shot very bright so they'll look normal on TV. And one other thing strikes you as very odd:

There are no ceilings! Since the sets are lit from above, the rooms are just walls. What's more, in order to give the big cameras room to move, the walls of each room aren't even all here! Just the ones that are going to be seen in a particular shot. You think to yourself how *amazing* it is that it all looks so real on TV!

Each room is built right next to another one—even if they're not on the same floor or even in the same building—just so it's easier to move the cameras from one to the other.

(One set that's *not* here is West Beverly Hills High. Most of the scenes set in the school are shot on location at Torrance High School.)

Unfortunately, because you were distracted by the def sets as you crossed the soundstage, you lost Jason. Quickly, you make your way behind the rooms of the Walsh house—stepping over the struts and sandbags that keep the fake walls from falling over—and go searching.

Chapter 3

There's a big garage-like door on the far side of the soundstage. It's open and leads outside, and you wonder if Jason went through there.

You hurry over, but before you can exit, you stop. You hear a familiar voice coming from around the corner. Your heart had *just* begun to slow down from the thrill of spending a few minutes with Jason, but now it's racing again.

Slowly, nervously, you step forward and poke your head out, peering into the dark shadow along the wall outside the soundstage.

Luke Perry is alone and walking briskly toward you, talking and gesturing as he approaches. He's talking about his relationship with Brenda Walsh, and whether she really thinks it'd be a good idea for him to come with them. (You don't know where they're going, but you think, *Yes! Who could turn Dylan down wherever they're going?*)

Has this hunky young man lost his marbles, muttering to himself like this?

Hardly! He's a serious actor running through his lines, making sure he knows them for the rest of the scenes that will be shot this morning.

Suddenly, he stops, opens a script that was rolled up under one arm, and checks the dialogue. He studies it in silence, and when he's got it right, he tucks the script back under his arm, then continues walking

15

toward the soundstage, reciting his lines.

He brushes past you, stops, and peers toward the set. When he sees that the director is still talking in the doorway, and everyone's still munching on their donuts, he says, "I thought I was gonna be *late*."

He's no longer Dylan McKay but Luke Perry—his voice gentler, his manner softer than when he was striding toward the soundstage.

Turning around, he spots you and, raising his index finger and thumb, "pops" you with his gun. He remembers you from a brief introduction earlier in the day, when a publicity representative for the show told him you'd be visiting the set. Incredibly, despite everything that's on his mind, he remembers *you* and takes the time to amble over.

"How's it been goin'?" he asks.

Your mouth is too dry to answer. When you were introduced earlier, there was no time to talk. Now he's standing here, actually *hanging* with you, and you can't form a single syllable.

You don't even know where to *look* first! Your eyes are drawn to the glinting gold earring he wears in his left ear—but then they wander over the entire long, lean, gorgeous face, the soulful eyes, the cool fifties hairstyle. Luke has been compared to everyone from the legendary teen idols James Dean and Matt Dillon to Vanilla Ice without the makeup and 'do.

But while there are similarities to each of those celebs, Luke's obviously his own man—lanky, nearly six feet tall, wearing a white T-shirt and jeans, with dark, smoldering eyes that stare out from under a high forehead. The sunken cheeks cause the ends of his mouth to turn up; he always looks like he's wearing a bemused smile.

When you can finally manage to utter a few words, you tell Luke that things couldn't be better, that everyone has been terrific to you, and how glad you are that all the gossip you've heard about the actors not getting along and being on ego trips is just reporters hissin' and dissin'. From everything you've seen, wealth and fame doesn't seem to have spoiled anyone.

"No," he says with a soft laugh, "it certainly hasn't." He rolls the script up in his hand and gestures toward the set.

He tells you that the success of *Beverly Hills, 90210* is a dream come true for all of them, and they couldn't be happier with the show *or* with each other. Luke says that the cast is like a family, and that while, sure, they may have an occasional difference of opinion over how to play a scene or deliver a line, that doesn't change the strong bond of love that exists between them all.

While he was talking, paying attention just to you, everything else on the soundstage seemed to disappear. (On the *soundstage? On the planet!*) Now a voice from behind brings you back to reality—much, much too soon!

Someone is calling Luke's name, but before he leaves he makes a point of telling you that he and Jason are *also* thankful for the love of their devoted fans. Without them, he says, the show could not have become the phenomenon it has.

He says he's looking forward to talking to you later, in his trailer.

As Luke walks away, you yell, "Wait!" surprised to hear yourself *shout* at one of the hottest, most powerful young stars in TV.

Your eyes widen and your mouth falls open in panic. You realize that Luke's charm is to blame for your boldness: he has so quickly put you at ease that you feel like he's someone you've known for years!

For a long, agonizing second, you wonder if he's going to have you thrown off the set. You've *heard* about how temperamental some stars can be. And you remember a couple of episodes where Dylan came dangerously close to the boiling point when people ticked him off . . .

But there's no attitude problem for *this* star. Luke turns and smiles, not the least bit bothered by your big, fat, gaping mouth.

"Yeesssss?" he says.

"I— I wanted to ask you a question," you stutter. "About Jason."

He shrugs. "Sure."

You realize that this is going to sound every bit as *dumb* as when you asked Jason the question, but you ask it anyway:

"Mr. Perry—"

"Luke," he gently corrects you.

"Uh . . . Luke, do you happen to know what part of Jason's body he wishes were different?"

The smile broadens and Luke laughs. "Yeah," he says. "All of it. He wishes he were me."

That's a brotherly swipe and you know it. You smile.

"Seriously," you say. "I asked him and he—"

"Luke!" a voice calls him again from the darkness.

"Gotta go," he says, heading back to the set. "Why don't you ask him?"

"I did—" you start to say, but Luke is jogging forward. Professional that he is, he doesn't want to hold anyone up.

You stand there for a moment, pondering the problem, then slowly walk toward the set yourself. You figure you're just going to have to wait for your answer, when suddenly the Man himself returns.

18

Chapter 4

Jason comes running through the big garage door behind you, a can of Diet Coke in one hand, his script in the other.

"Hi," he says as he passes.

"Wait!" you cry and start jogging after him.

"I'm late!" he says as he heads back toward the set.

You know he won't stop and talk now, so, sighing, you follow him toward the set, where rehearsals and filming are about to resume.

When they rehearse, the actors work on the set, scripts in hand, simultaneously reading and memorizing their lines under the watchful eye of the director, who sits on a chair directly in front of the set. While the actors work, the camera operators do their *own* rehearsal, figuring out where they have to move to shoot the scene the way the director wants.

The scene they're doing now is set in Brenda Walsh's bedroom. Picking up a script that belongs to an assistant director, you take a peek and learn that in this episode, the Walsh kids and their friends are going camping in the Yosemite Valley.

At the last minute, Dylan has been invited to come along, and he agrees. That means Brenda has to do some repacking, and while she's busy doing that, Dylan drops by her bedroom.

Jason is standing off to the side, practicing flipping his hat up his forearm and onto his head, something he's decided to do in a scene that will be filmed later. Actress Shannen Doherty is already on the set, having stayed behind to study her own lines during the short break. She's sitting on a folding director's chair with her name on the back.

Shannen is even more radiant in person than she seems on TV (which is *very* radiant). Her hair is glossy, and her skin is fair and very smooth. (You learn later that part of that is due to an electric massager she uses, one which removes all kinds of bacteria from the skin.) And Shannen's big smile is a mankiller: it's easy to understand why Dylan McKay fell so hard for her!

Now that it's time to get to work, Shannen gets up, walks into Brenda's room, plunks the script by the duffel bag on the bed, stops biting her nails (a habit she hates but can't seem to break), and stands by the bed, stuffing clothes into the bag.

Luke checks the script one more time, then sets it on a small table at the foot of the bed, near where he'll be standing.

The actors are in place; the crew is set. Director Melman tells them to start.

Dylan swaggers into the room and asks Brenda if she needs a hand. Then he gets serious: he wonders if it's really a good idea to come along (so *this* is the scene Luke was rehearsing as he walked toward the soundstage). After all, he says, their relationship has been going through some strange times lately.

Like just about any sane girl on the planet, Brenda tells her moody boyfriend that *of course* he should come along: it'll be good for him to get away with some good friends. Reluctantly, Luke agrees to go.

The director tells them to do it again, but this time to try it a little differently: he wants Luke to be a little more compassionate when they talk about how the relationship will have to be *platonic* for a few days.

Even though it's late morning and they've been here

20

since five-thirty—and will probably still be here at dinnertime and possibly as late as ten o'clock at night—Luke and Shannen gladly do the scene again. Not only do the actors want each and every episode to be as good as it can be, but both Luke and Shannen obviously don't mind in the *least* having to go through it all over again. The chemistry they have together is real and very exciting.

And they don't mind doing the scene *again* when the director wants to try it another way. And then another way. And then a fifth way.

Fame . . . money . . . *and* close camaraderie on the set! You wonder how life could possibly be any better for the young stars of *Beverly Hills, 90210*.

Yet, as good as things are for them, and especially for Luke and Jason, you know they didn't get here just on their good looks and talent alone (though it obviously didn't hurt to have gobs of both).

No, Jason Priestley and Luke Perry got where they are thanks to years of hard work. There were acting lessons, literally hundreds of auditions for all *kinds* of parts, and bearing up under the constant rejection that every actor must endure.

Even *after* they landed the roles, there was the incredible pressure that haunts the cast of every show in the weeks before it goes on the air:

Are we doing *everything* we can to make this show a hit? Are we working hard enough to make our characters believable? Likable? Could the stories be more interesting?

How will people react to us when we do interviews on TV, in magazines and newspapers, make personal appearances in malls? (If they'd *only* known . . .)

How will *we* react to people, to fellow members of the cast as well as reporters and fans? What will we do if the show's a hit and photographers snap our pictures when we come out of restaurants, arrive at airports, or

21

even go to the dentist to have our teeth cleaned?

The rewards are great, but, as you can tell, so are the pressures.

Fortunately, despite their youth, both Jason and Luke were seasoned pros before they checked into the 90210 zip code, pros who were uniquely suited to handle these and other, unexpected responsibilities!

Chapter 5

Forget about your *first* question for Jason for a moment, the crazy one about his body parts. Ask Jason Bradford Priestley where he was born.

Go ahead, make his day.

You're sitting with him in his trailer during lunch, and he *dares* you to ask him. And when you take the bait (who could resist such a way cool star?) he sits back, folds his hands on his waist, and tells you with *all* seriousness that he was born in primitive Borneo, the son of a squid fisherman.

"Were you really?" you ask.

Only then does he grin with satisfaction at having *clocked* you, and says no, he was born in Vancouver, British Columbia, one of the largest and most beautiful seaports in Canada.

One thing you quickly learn about Jason Priestley is that he *loves* to kid his friends, his coworkers, and especially casual acquaintances. (Why *especially* casual acquaintances? Because, he says, they never know what to expect from him, so they're easier to fool!)

However, something *else* you discover about Jason is that once he gets serious, he tends to be very, *very* serious. When he's talking about his work and about his life, he doesn't joke. Unlike many stars, he also doesn't fudge facts and tell outright lies. When Jason talks, you can be sure he's giving you as honest an answer as he can.

Jason was born on August 28, 1969, the second child of Sharon and Lorne Priestley. (Donnie Wahlberg, River Phoenix, Michael Jackson, Christian Slater, and Patrick Swayze were all born in the same month . . . but who rules?)

For as long as Jason can remember, he says, he got along *very* well with his sister, Justine, who was born just a year and a half before him. He also loved growing up in Vancouver, which is on the west coast of Canada and "is such a beautiful place," he says. "It can get cold and rainy, but I love it."

His mother, Sharon, did a great deal of professional acting, and Jason got his first taste of show business when she was acting in the movie *That Cold Day in the Park*. This was shortly after Jason was born, and when the script called for a baby in one scene, you-know-who was cast.

"Right at the beginning of the movie," Jason smiles, "there's a shot of a baby crying—and that's me!" He admits, "I've never seen the movie, but that was my first film role."

He's never seen it? Jason says he doesn't even remember *making* the film. But he *does* remember being two and three years old and accompanying his mother when she worked on other film and TV shows and on the stage, and says that he soon realized "There was performing in my blood." And when Jason was four years old, he came to the conclusion that he, too, wanted to act professionally.

"Mind you," says Jason, "my mother was not the stage mother type who wanted to push me into it like many do. She was very cool about my career."

Cool? She was positively astounded when the precocious little boy walked over to her one night and asked if she would mind if he took acting lessons and tried out for TV commercials.

24

Sharon knew that Jason was serious, because he had always been very serious about *everything*, whether it was work or play. But she also knew that an acting career would be a big commitment on *both* of their parts.

Still, she decided to help him and was proud of her son, thinking, how many four-year-olds are ready to accept responsibilities like that?

Sharon made only one provision before agreeing to help little Jason. In order to make sure he understood that what he was getting involved in was serious business and not play, she told him that as soon as he started earning money, he'd have to pay for her to drive him to and from auditions.

Jason smiles when he says that when he *did* start earning money, "I asked her, 'Why do I have to pay you?' and she said, 'Well, if I didn't drive you, you'd have to take a cab and you'd have to pay the cab driver.' "

Jason says that that was a wise thing for her to do, for it not only taught him the importance of making a commitment to something and *sticking with it*, it also taught him the value of money. You couldn't just squander it on things you wanted: first came the things you *needed*.

Four-year-old Jason started by trying out for what he calls "silly things." Because he was so cute and outgoing, and a naturally talented actor, he started getting parts almost right away, which is *very* good for a young boy without much training: he acted in commercials for fruit juice, lunch meat, dog food, toy trucks, "and all that kind of stuff."

His proudest achievement of this period was starring in a made-for-Canadian-TV movie when he was eight, a delightful little film called *Stacey*.

However, after a little over four years in the business, Jason realized that because of all the time he was spending going to auditions after school, his boyhood was passing him by.

Deciding to retire and just "be a regular kid" for a while, he stopped acting so he could live a normal childhood—participating in sports, taking up an instrument (he selected the drums), and just hanging with other kids.

Chapter 6

Jason successfully got into the swing of a "normal" life, and was a happy kid throughout junior and senior high school—though he admits that the best thing about school was "the strong friendships I made," and not the classes, which he didn't *really* like.

(Though he can't resist joking that he spent part of his high school career in reform school with a lot of knife-wielding toughs—which is why he's such a cutup today.)

But don't think that Jason was a bad student: he wasn't. He always got very good grades, though that was *not* because he went home and crammed each night. He was naturally bright and knowledge came easily to him.

The truth is, while he hated studying just to memorize facts, a big part of him really wanted to learn. As a result, though Jason didn't study a lot, he *did* read every night—the kinds of things that interested *him*. These were mostly novels, ranging from the classics to modern books like *A Clockwork Orange* (a frightening tale about a bunch of teenage thugs in a dreary world of the future).

Even today, Jason never goes anywhere without a book in his backpack.

He also asked a *lot* of questions in class. He says with a laugh, "Yeah, I questioned *everything*. I found out that the secret to learning is questioning what you're hearing, instead of just taking in facts."

Questioning also took the form of little rebellious acts. Early in his high school career, Jason confesses, "I jumped onto the tail end of the punk movement," and took to wearing "chains, black jeans, combat boots," the works. Once, he even shaved his hair *real* short (like just a millimeter less than *bald*).

He laughs, describing himself as having been "the rebel without a clue when I was in high school," and admits he was uncomfortable doing something just because it was a trend, just because the other kids were doing it.

After a few years, he got off that roller coaster and only did the things that made sense to him—whether it was fashionable or not. And you know what he found? That the people who really mattered to him liked him for himself!

Jason spent his free time going out with friends. Of course, they went to the movies a *lot*, and Jason made a point of never missing *anything* starring Robert Duvall, Al Pacino, James Woods, or Dennis Hopper. He was (and still is) absolutely *hypnotized* by their films.

When they weren't sitting in the movies, Jason and his friends listened to music (the performer Jason has always enjoyed to the max, above and beyond everyone else, is rocker Elvis Costello) or went out and consumed vast quantities of hamburgers and french fries.

Together, Jason and his close bunch of pals would talk about their dreams for the future, their girlfriends— and also play practical jokes on each other (bet *that* doesn't come as a big surprise!).

They'd also do a little bird-watching (bet that *does* come as a surprise; their beauty and freedom has always fascinated Jason), or talk about Jason's three sports/outdoorsy passions: riding motorcycles (Yamahas in particular) and playing rugby or ice hockey (at which he is very, very good).

All of these love affairs, from the burgers to hockey to motorcycling, continue to this day.

And speaking of love affairs, Jason says he had puh-*lenty* of them in high school. He went from one crush to another (news flash: he *never* had any trouble finding girls who had a crush on *him*), and was sure that each and every girl he dated was the one he wanted to marry.

However, he realizes today that each relationship was only a healthy infatuation and nothing more. "You think you fall in love every week," he says about high school, "but you really don't know what love is." At least, he says *he* didn't. Otherwise, he could never have changed girlfriends several times a month!

Something else that surfaced during Jason's high school days, and is one of the most important aspects of his life today, is *fair play*.

Jason was always the first kid to leap to the defense of someone who was being picked on, and he believes in fighting for the rights of everyone to have their own opinions—regardless of how they conflict with those of anyone else, including him.

He says that a lot of "bad karma" comes from hate and prejudice, and he doesn't like to see it or experience it in any form.

In fact, he says that one of his hopes is that he can use his influence as an actor to encourage tolerance, whether through personal appearances or by the kinds of shows and movies he makes.

Chapter 7

Despite the fact that Jason was involved in so many things during high school, the acting bug never left his blood. Even when he was in tenth grade, he says, "I started to think about what I wanted to do with my life. And I figured that acting was it."

Actually, when Jason was fifteen years old, he was torn between *two* careers: becoming an actor or a professional ice hockey player. However, after sitting down with his parents and talking it over, he realized he wasn't tall or brawny enough to get on the ice and mix it up with the bruisers of the NHL. (Just imagine if he'd tried out for the sport and caught a hockey puck in the mouth. Can you *bear* the thought of Jason with a *toothless* smile?)

So the young man decided to pursue acting. Just as when he was four years old, never once was he intimidated by the odds against him. He knew he would never be happy if he abandoned his dream and pursued a life and career he didn't love.

The first thing Jason did was to make time in his life to start studying acting seriously. And since Mr. Priestley *never* does anything halfway, he ended up taking six different courses—*all at the same time*!

He remembers, "I really got into studying theater. I took classes all over town and absorbed everything I could."

(When did he sleep? He says he didn't—and still

doesn't—*need* that much sleep. Jason has always had an abundance of energy and, besides, there's just too much he always wants to *do*.)

During this time, Jason met a person who had an enormous impact on his life: June Whitaker, an acting coach and a founding member of the prestigious Neighborhood Playhouse.

Jason says that she's a "really amazing" teacher *and* person. She recognized his talent and ambition and nurtured it with love and enthusiasm.

"She brought out so many feelings and skills in me," he says fondly, "emotions and talents that I never even knew I was capable of! No matter how much she taught me, she always had more to give."

The key to June's teaching technique was to allow Jason to try all different kinds of acting styles. She taught him how to interpret lines in different and interesting ways, how to improvise, and how to react to what other actors were saying. She showed him how to use his body: how to act with a glance instead of words, use his hands for emphasis, present his back to the audience, and suggest a mood or emotion using his posture.

"I'd sometimes find that a method really worked well for me," Jason says, and he would make that part of his acting style. Today, when you watch him on TV, a lot of the gestures and inflections you're seeing are things that June Whitaker taught him. Obviously, he didn't have the same trouble paying attention to *her* that he did picking up facts and figures in school!

Jason studied with June until the end of his high school career, after which he threw himself back into auditioning with the fury of an NHL power play. He went out for commercials, for TV shows, and for motion pictures—everything and anything that came along.

The young man's credentials as a child actor were of no use to him now, and not surprisingly, the first few months were filled with disappointment. Not only did he go on a lot of auditions and not get many parts, but the process of auditioning itself can be a long and discouraging one.

First you have to impress the casting agents, the people who select the handful of actors to present to the director. Then, if you get a "call-back" to see the director (or for the casting agents to have another look at you) and are fortunate enough to impress that person, you usually get *another* call-back so they can check you out again . . . and sometimes a *third* call-back after that to make sure the chemistry's right between you and any actors they've already chosen for parts. (Wait'll you hear how many times Luke Perry had to go back before *he* got his *Beverly Hills, 90210* role!)

It's a long process in which your hopes go up and down more often than a mall elevator.

But Jason says that just starting out and *not* getting parts was in many ways more useful than getting them.

Sound strange? Not at all! He says he learned that "if you stick it out and if you can keep working—take the disappointment and the rejection and keep going and keep your focus and drive—then I think you can rise above it."

And rise above it he did.

Boy, how he did.

Chapter 8

At first, Jason wanted to work in Canada as much as possible. Not only did he believe strongly in the Canadian film and TV industry, but his family was there and he didn't want to be far from them.

But back in 1986, there weren't nearly as many shows and feature films being shot in Canada as there are today. That growth wouldn't come until about two years later, when producers realized that not only is it less expensive to film in Canada, but the scenery isn't as familiar as all of those locales in sunny Southern California.

Jason knew that in order to survive he'd have to do at least *some* work in Hollywood, and it was a realization that proved prophetic: no sooner was he committed to going wherever the jobs were, than he landed a small part in the made-for-TV movie *Nobody's Child*, which was based on a true-life story. The highly rated film starred Marlo Thomas in an Emmy Award–winning role as Marie Balter, a mental patient who struggles to convince her doctors that she's capable of leading a normal life.

Jason went to Southern California to play a character listed only as "2nd Boy" in the credits—but, as they say in show business, at least it was a TV credit! And he had a great time meeting Marlo Thomas, who he thought was super.

Jason followed that part with another, a small role in the TV movie *Lies from Lotus Land*.

Making off with the Triple Crown, he also got a motion picture part that same year, 1986—the first theatrical film since his now-famous crying baby debut! This time he played Gary in *The Boy Who Could Fly*, a film about a new girl in a small town who becomes friends with an autistic boy. The movie starred an even younger actor who made good, Fred Savage, and also starred Bonnie Bedelia (Bruce Willis's wife in the *Die Hard* movies), Colleen Dewhurst, Fred Gwynne (best known as Herman Munster), and Academy Award winner Louise Fletcher.

Though Jason's part was once again extremely small, it was important to him not only because he got to work with these experienced pros, but also because for the first time he saw how really big stars conduct themselves on-screen and off. Jason recalls that all of them were very courteous to him *and* to their fans.

It was a lesson he'd never forget. He vowed that if *he* ever became famous, he would act just as kindly as they had.

Unfortunately, when he went back to Canada, there was still not a lot of work. He continued to audition for parts, but began to realize that if he were going to make a living at this, he was going to have to go on many, many more calls, get his face seen (and remembered) by more casting agents, try out for *everything* he could.

Thus, late in 1986, Jason came to the difficult decision that he was going to have to move to where the action was, which in this case was Hollywood, U.S.A.

Jason recalls, "I felt to really do the kind of projects I wanted to and get the kind of parts I wanted and do the things that would satisfy me creatively, that's where I had to be."

He also felt he should try to find an acting coach who would take him beyond what he'd done with June: who could teach him as much about acting for a camera as June had for the stage.

There *are* differences in the techniques: for example, on-stage, where you're far from the audience, your gestures have to be very big and broad. You have to learn how to project your voice.

On-camera, you can communicate emotions in more subtle ways, such as the raising of an eyebrow—something Jason has come to do oh-so-well.

Also, you speak differently on-stage than on-camera. When you're acting for TV, you don't have to send your voice to the last row of the balcony!

Naturally, Hollywood was the place to learn that, too, so there were now *two* good reasons to go.

While it's pretty amazing that Jason has risen so far so fast, it's important not to lose sight of the sheer *guts* he had coming to Los Angeles as a seventeen-year-old.

Vancouver is a big city, but it's civilized and clean. Los Angeles isn't like that: it's packed with traffic, noise and smog, and thousands upon thousands of young, sometimes desperate people all trying to make it in the same business.

Mind you, there *are* beautiful parts of the city, too, but you've got to have mucho money to live in them—and that was one thing Jason *didn't* have. He'd saved up some money from the movies he'd done and from his years of acting in commercials (after paying back his chauffeur mom, of course).

But it wasn't a *ton* of money, and he figured he could survive in Los Angeles for a year without getting a single part—which, even considering his talent, training, and drop-dead good looks, was a distinct possibility. A great deal of luck is also needed to make it in the business, and you can't really plan on that!

The trick was, he had to find a cheap place to live—
a *very* cheap place to live—but one that was still close
enough to the studios and casting agencies so he could
go for auditions.

Chapter 9

Jason found the perfect place to live: a very small apartment in North Hollywood, a cheerful community of closely packed homes and straight, tree-lined streets. He shared the place with another aspiring actor, and to get around, the guys got themselves an old car, a 1968 Cadillac Coupe DeVille, which they nicknamed "Homesmobile."

Jason also found an acting teacher who took his talent and polished it to a high sheen. The teacher's name was Howard Fine, and Jason says the instructor really worked hard to teach him about TV and movie acting, and also how to "emotionally prepare myself before I attempt a scene."

That was important, because getting into the right frame of mind quickly and correctly is crucial when you only have a few days to shoot a TV show. And that ability, more than anything else, has become the key to Jason's riveting acting style.

"I put myself in the mood and really live out the situation," he says. "I know many performers who take a long time to get themselves into the right emotional state to act, but I'm fortunate not to have that problem. I have what you might call free-flowing emotions."

At first, things looked like they were only going to go *right* for Jason.

Almost at once, he landed the starring role as Buzz in the serial *Teen Angel*, which was inspired by the

1959 rock and roll hit. The mini-series aired as part of the new *Mickey Mouse Club* show on cable TV's The Disney Channel.

His coworkers remember him as very good, very cooperative, very generous with his costars, and very eager to make sure the TV movie was a success. Even *they* predicted fame and fortune for the lad.

But in 1987, The Disney Channel didn't have as many subscribers as it does today, and the film went largely unnoticed. Jason's hopes that the movie would jump-start his Hollywood career were dashed.

And there was more bad news waiting just around the corner. Food, gas, clothes (you've got to look good for auditions!), and even the apartment were much more expensive than Jason had anticipated, and he says that he spent his savings "at an incredible rate." In just a few months, he says, "I had no money."

So what did he do when the funds ran dangerously low? (Apart from giving up the big, fat, juicy, *expensive* hamburgers at the Sunset Boulevard eateries and settling for fast-food burgers?) He spent even *more* time in his car, trying out for every acting job he could, whether it was movies, commercials, or little stage plays.

Still, it was "no go" everywhere he turned. There was talk about a sequel to *Teen Angel*, but that was put on hold, and he came close to getting a few parts. However, "close" doesn't pay the bills. He actually started *living* in his car to save money.

Jason was disappointed, of course, but not discouraged. He was *still* doing what he wanted: he was free and getting experience in sunny L.A. More than once he told himself at least he was *on* the Yellow Brick Road looking for the Wizard. Not many people even get to do that.

In fact, he says, "I look back on it now and it was the most fun I ever had in my life." All of his options were still open, his future spread before him, and he *knew* he'd eventually get a break.

And he admits that one thought above all kept him going, a point of pride: he told himself that if fellow young Canadian Michael J. Fox (Fox even hailed from Vancouver also) could make it in Hollywood, so could he!

Ultimately, though, after the year was up and the only thing in his wallet was photos of the family, Jason had no choice but to reach a very unhappy decision: he was going to have to pack up his belongings and head back north, to Vancouver.

But you know Jason: he didn't regard it as a defeat, just as a temporary setback. He still intended to make acting his career, and he knew he'd be coming back to Hollywood somehow, and soon.

But even Jason would have been surprised to learn *how* soon!

Chapter 10

Returning home, Jason was glad to have the loving support of his parents and sister: though he'd spoken to them regularly on the phone when he was in Hollywood, he hadn't realized how much he'd missed their encouragement and their friendly, affectionate faces.

Like Popeye gulping down spinach, he found their love energizing! In fact, Jason even suggested once—as a joke, natch—that he and sib Justine come up with a comedy act spoofing Alex Keaton and Mallory Keaton of *Family Ties*. (Ironically, his sister has the same first name as Justine "Mallory" Bateman!)

However, Justine Priestley wisely dissed and dismissed *that* kooky idea.

Jason's *real* plan was to try to work in Canadian commercials, films, and TV again, save up some money, and make another assault on Hollywood. He still believed he could make it, and refused to give up the dream.

However, things didn't quite work out the way Jason planned. (Do they *ever* for him?)

The young actor was just wrapping up his first fruitless six months back in Vancouver when he got a call from an agent to come *back* to Los Angeles and try out for a part.

It wasn't a *big* part—playing a kid in a horror

movie called *Watchers*—but it was money *and* it was Hollywood.

Racking up those frequent flyer miles, Jason went back to L.A., auditioned, and got the role—his first theatrical motion picture part since becoming a full-time professional actor!

Watchers, a creepy flick starring Corey Haim, opened and closed in one week in 1988 and was a big-time bomb for everyone involved—*except* Jason. He says he can't even find the words to describe the sheer joy he felt at taking another small step forward in his career.

With the money he earned from the film, Jason decided to stay in Hollywood. Instead of the gas guzzler he'd driven around before, however, he bought an inexpensive motorcycle to get about and started making the rounds again. And lo and behold . . .

In the beginning of 1989, things really began to cook for the twenty-year-old actor. No—not because of the hot-looking Yamaha. Casting agents were finally taking note of the outrageously good-looking actor (he'd matured since they last saw him), and suddenly, almost everyone in Tinseltown was chasin' amazin' Jason.

The sequel to *Teen Angel* finally got off the ground, called (surprise!) *Teen Angel Returns*. In the first film, Jason played a guardian angel who helps a shy high school student impress the girl of his dreams. In the sequel, he helps a lovely young girl (you'll never guess who played her!) gain confidence and out-smart a mall developer.

He also played a kid named Howard in a stinkeroo theatrical film called *Nowhere to Run*. (How bad was the movie? Like *Watchers*, within days after it opened it was nowhere to be found!)

Jase also started guest-starring in episodes of many, many TV series, and if you tune into reruns you'll be able to catch him in *MacGyver, Quantum Leap, 21 Jump Street*, and *Airwolf*, among many others.

41

Man, were things cooking—even though a lot of these characters weren't exactly the kinds of people Jason wanted to play.

He says that during this period, "I used to play bad guy..." He pauses and grins. "Really *hard*, bad guys." (Tough to believe, isn't it, considering what a *good* guy Brandon is. Just goes to show what a dynamite actor Jason is!)

But he wasn't complaining. In fact, with money in his pocket and more and more experience under his belt, he couldn't have been much happier.

Yet an even bigger break occurred in the summer of 1989.

He had tried out for continuing roles in TV series before, and nothing had ever come of it. So he didn't expect much when he went out for another one—this time, the part of Todd in a brand-new NBC-TV pilot, *Sister Kate*.

But after an audition and two call-backs, he was startled to get a call from his agent saying that he'd gotten the part: that day marked the last time in his life that Jason Priestley would *ever* be unemployed.

Chapter 11

A pilot is a sample show the networks order when they like a script and want to see how the show will look *before* they order thirteen episodes (which is the usual number they buy).

Jason shot the pilot, and a few weeks went by before he got the word: NBC loved the show and wanted to put it into production as a series.

He was hyper-excited now, though there wasn't time to savor his incredible good fortune: the network wanted the producers to start shooting immediately. Jason picked up the first script and started rehearsals a few days later.

One really nice thing about the deal: NBC scheduled *Sister Kate* to follow *The Magical World of Disney* on the Sunday night lineup, making Jason feel like he was still a part of the Disney family, sort of.

Sister Kate was a half-hour comedy set in Redemption House, a Catholic home for children. There, the tough-as-nails Sister Kate (Stephanie Beacham, an English actress best known for her previous role as Sable Scott Colby on *The Colbys*) looked after seven independent orphans: seven-year-old Neville (Jole Robinson), nine-year-old Violet (Alexaundria Simmons), eleven-year-old Eugene (Harley Cross), twelve-year-old wheelchair-bound Hillary (Penina Segall), and sixteen-year-olds Freddy (Hannah Cutrona), April (Erin Reed)—and hip, smart-alecky Todd (Jason), whose biggest interest is girls, even though (if you can believe this!) he has a lot of trouble getting them to be interested in him!

The show debuted on September 24, 1989, at eight o'clock, after two previews had been aired on the sixteenth and twenty-first in an effort to build interest in the show.

Jason was *really* excited about *Sister Kate*'s chances for success. He was confident that the subject of the show, the humor and warmth, and the endearing characters would win it a loyal following.

He was also incredibly excited by the thought that after years of being seen by relatively small numbers of people, he'd be coming into the homes of at least ten million people every Sunday night!

But, once again, things didn't go as planned.

The Magical World of Disney was on opposite the incredibly popular *60 Minutes*. Despite having the Disney name, it was a big, big failure. Even worse: people watching *60 Minutes* on CBS stayed tuned for *Murder, She Wrote*.

The very successful mystery show was in its fifth season, and though NBC did a lot of promotion, they just couldn't get people to tune in to see Jason Priestley instead of Angela Lansbury. It's a strange world.

Even Jason's appearance in the widely seen special *Hollywood Christmas Parade* failed to attract attention to the show.

Sister Kate was pulled from the schedule in January of 1990. (Though you can bet your pumps that NBC will be bringing back those old shows to cash in on Jason's newfound fame!)

Well—there was good news for Jason in that he'd earned thousands of dollars per episode, so he had enough money to hold on in Hollywood for quite a while.

44

Still, as anyone can certainly understand, that didn't stop him from being terribly upset when the network pulled the rug out from under the show. As with all his projects, he'd put his heart into *Sister Kate*. And after spending months with the other cast members, day in and day out, he'd grown very close to them. This was especially true with the older kids, who had talked about their dreams and had even gotten into the Priestley habit of playing practical jokes on one another.

Jason had also enjoyed working with one director in particular and was *convinced* they'd never get to work together again . . . a guy by the name of Jeff Melman!

Now, all of a sudden, it was over, and they all had to go their separate ways.

That's a part of the industry all actors have to face, but this was the first time Jason had experienced it, and he found it very depressing. He genuinely *likes* people and grows especially close to fellow actors when he's working with them.

And because he's so sensitive, he not only hurt for himself, but for the other kids on *Sister Kate* as well, who were all just as disappointed as he was.

But, as everyone in show business knows, regardless of how a series or movie does, life goes on and actors move on.

Jason did a smart thing then: he joined a weekend hockey league in Los Angeles to keep up his spirits and to build the kind of friendships that *couldn't* be separated by the whim of a network executive.

He plays center in the division-two hockey league, which means that he gets to face-off against professional hockey players, who use his team for practice. Often, says the self-effacing Jason, the pros use his team's *sticks* for toothpicks . . . meaning that, try as they might, it's tough for Jason and his fellow weekend warriors to beat the established players. But he says he'll never stop trying . . . in fact, he even did a scene in a recent *90210* episode wearing rollerblades and practicing his slapshots.

Something else that helped him get through this unhappy period was his motorcycle. He says he'd "get out of L.A. and go up into the mountains." There, he tried not to think bad thoughts, but to reflect on how *lucky* he was to have come this far in so short a time.

This feeling was reinforced by his mother, who knew—from hard experience—that when you choose acting as a career, you can't afford to have thin skin!

Fortunately, the next time Jason stepped in front of a camera—just a few weeks later—the results were considerably different!

Chapter 12

For forty years, the three TV networks—CBS, ABC, and (boo!) NBC—dominated the airwaves. They had the money, the affiliates (stations that aired their shows in each city), and strong relationships with the Hollywood producers who make TV shows.

But in 1987, Barry Diller, the head of the Twentieth Century-Fox movie studio, felt there was room for a fourth network, a network with *different* kinds of programs. Shows aimed at young people; hipper, more unusual, more topical, and faster-paced programs than the ones on the stodgy old networks.

Fox set aside a bunch of money to fund the new undertaking, and signed up affiliates that were not attached to any network (the kind of stations that show only local programs, syndicated shows like *Oprah*, or reruns of network shows).

In its first year of operation, Fox only had shows on two nights, Saturday and Sunday (as opposed to the four nights they have now).

The Saturday night lineup was a Titanic-sized disaster: does anyone even *remember* the shows *Mr. President, Women in Prison, New Adventures of Beans Baxter,* and *Second Chance*? (Barry Diller probably doesn't even remember them, except in nightmares!)

However, Sunday night was a different matter. The lineup consisted of *Werewolf, Married . . . with Children, The Tracey Ullman Show* (featuring the

Simpsons), *Duet*, and one other show: an hour-long series called *21 Jump Street*, about four young police officers who worked undercover in Los Angeles schools.

21 Jump Street was a big, instant hit, and made believers of the people who thought the Fox Network couldn't possibly compete against the big boys.

Part of the show's success was due to its storylines, which dealt with hot topics like drugs, sex, prejudice, and other situations faced by big city teenagers.

However, as the weeks went on and the ratings climbed, Diller didn't need a billboard on Sunset Boulevard to tell him that the *real* reason people were tuning in was to see cool, sexy young Johnny Depp, who starred as Officer Tom Hanson. (Depp's subsequent success as the star of movies like *Cry Baby* and *Edward Scissorhands* and the upcoming *The Arrowtooth Waltz* shows what good taste Fox's audience had!)

Diller put the word out in Hollywood, among the producers, that Fox would be *very* interested in looking at ideas for other shows that featured handsome, young teensomethings.

Enter Darren Star, a thirty-year-old who had never come up with a TV show in his life.

But he had an idea.

"In high school everything is so important and serious," he says. Yet, he realized, "there wasn't a show that addressed that mindset."

His idea was to come up with a series which did that, but in a special way. He remembered how viewers in the early 1960s used to love the old series *The Beverly Hillbillies*, which was about a simple, country family who struck it rich and suddenly found themselves living in one of the ritziest places in America.

The Beverly Hillbillies was a half-hour comedy. Star's notion was to do an hour-long drama in which an ordinary family of four from the Midwest is forced

48

to move to Beverly Hills. Instead of *jokes* about the cultural differences between the old and new, as on *The Beverly Hillbillies*, he'd show the serious problems the family would have to face in their new, cutting-edge setting.

Like *21 Jump Street*, the show would deal with the very real issues of teenage sex, drug abuse, romance, date rape, AIDS, divorce, drunk driving, peer pressure, and other contemporary problems.

Chapter 13

What Star came up with was the saga of the Walsh
family.

When a big, international accounting firm trans-
fers father Jim from its Minneapolis branch to the
Los Angeles office, the family is forced to leave
snowy, relaxed, clean, and conservative Minneapolis,
Minnesota, for sun-drenched, wet-and-wild, trendy
Southern California. (Something Jason could definitely
relate to!)

The Walsh family consists of two parents and two
teens. The parents are kind and devoted, down-to-
earth mother Cindy and hardworking Jim, both of
whom are trying to preserve their family's close bond
and wholesome values in their disorienting, sometimes mad new world. The teens are sixteen-year-old
twins Brandon and his three-minutes-younger sister,
Brenda.

Star conceived of Brandon and Brenda as being very
close and loving, but they're also different in several
important ways.

Though they both come to the Los Angeles area and
the fictional West Beverly High School—where they're
juniors—with fairly traditional Midwestern values,
Brandon holds on to those values far more tightly
and successfully than his sister does.

Brandon is the kind of teen who would (and eventually does, on the show) help the homeless or actually

50

run away from the advances of an immoral young woman. He was very popular back in Minnesota, but here he's outclassed by the Beverly Hills brats and he has to work hard to fit in . . . even though he's not always sure that he wants to. (Also remarkably like the teenaged Jason!) Even though Brandon is very hip in many ways, he's incredibly naive in many other ways.

Brenda, on the other hand, only *talks* like a conservative, generally to please her parents. In reality, she's become very much a part of the Beverly Hills social whirl—far more successfully and *easily* than her brother has. She's also much less shy about physical relationships, part of which is due to the incredibly powerful influence of . . .

The bad-egg boyfriend Star came up with for Brenda, Dylan McKay. A recovering alcoholic, a ladykiller, and the product of a broken home, Dylan brings a *different* kind of cultural shock right smack into the Walsh family living room. Instead of being snooty and rich, he's blunt, honest, and more than a little cynical—qualities that usually put him at odds with the other teens.

(Interestingly, Star didn't create Dylan right away. Everyone's favorite social outcast was written into the script just a month before the first show was to be filmed. Seems Star and the producers realized that all of the kids on the show were too good or too clean looking. Even though they were all different, someone was needed who *stood out* . . . so Star created Dylan.)

The other characters Star dreamed up were Brenda's friends Kelly Taylor, who is the popular leader-of-the-chic-clique but emotionally insecure; Donna Martin, sassy and upscale; timid but super-smart Andrea Zuckerman, Brandon's sort-of girlfriend; fun-loving class deejay and class clown David Silver, who pals around with Brandon; spoiled and often obnoxious high

51

society snob Steve Sanders, the not-very-responsible son of a hotshot movie actress; and outsider Scott Scott, who is bright but even more socially naive than Brandon.

Figuring that Fox would be a perfect place for the series, Star decided to take it to them early in 1990 and *bingo!* His instincts were right.

Fox bought the show and decided to put it right into production—like, right away, so it would be ready for the fall season. But first, they had to take care of two small problems:

Find an experienced producer and good writers and directors who could make the show something really special, and . . .

Find actors for the show, especially a Brandon and a Dylan who had the potential to become the next Johnny Depp.

Chapter 14

When it came time to choose someone to oversee the creative team of the new show—story editors, writers, producers, and directors—a casual observer *might* have thought that the people at Fox had gone just a little bananas.

Did the studio turn to some righteous music video producer or some slick, young hotshot to produce the show?

Uh-uh.

Did they ask a hot young film director to try his or her hand at a TV series (the way David Lynch had done with *Twin Peaks*)?

Nope.

They asked soft-spoken, veteran television producer Aaron Spelling if he wanted the job.

Mr. Spelling has been a *very* successful producer since the 1960s, and his string of smashes has included such monster hits as *The Mod Squad, Charlie's Angels, The Love Boat*, and *Dynasty*.

Still, Mr. Spelling is sixty-eight years old—definitely *not* a youngster, not a member of the MTV generation the show would have to appeal to.

Would he know what to do with the show? Would he know *how* to reach the youth audience?

You bet! Not only has he *always* known what appeals to viewers, but he is a father himself and knew exactly what his then-seventeen-year-old daughter liked and didn't like. And he'd produced the much-praised, very sensitive hour-long drama *Family*, which proved that he could handle personal relationships as well as fun and glitz!

So he was right for the job. The question was, did Mr. Spelling even *want* the job? (He was already one of the richest men in Hollywood!)

At first, he most certainly did not. When Fox made the offer, Mr. Spelling said that he didn't want to do a wacky kind of show like *Ferris Bueller's Day Off* or *Parker Lewis Can't Lose*. He also didn't want to do a series about a bunch of spoiled rich kids in a Beverly Hills school. He felt that with all the problems kids have to deal with today, TV programs should have more substance than that.

Much to his delight, Fox agreed with him one hundred percent!

Mr. Spelling recalls, "They said, 'No, no, we'd like to do a show in Beverly Hills, with strangers from Minnesota coming to it.' I said, *'That's* intriguing.'"

After thinking about all the possibilities, Mr. Spelling says, "I really got excited."

To make sure the show was both as realistic and as good as it could be, Fox also signed writer and executive producer Charles Rosin—one of the creative forces behind the popular and award-winning *Northern Exposure*, who had also written some powerful made-for-TV movies like *The Morris Dees Story*, about the civil rights worker, and *Summer Dreams*, the story of the rock group the Beach Boys. He was a hip *and* topical writer!

(He was also smart: to serve as the series' story editors—the folks who work with the writers to make sure each script is as brilliant as it can be—he brought in husband-and-wife writers Steve Wasserman and Jessica Klein, who had also written for *Northern Exposure*.)

And to direct the first show, Mr. Spelling hired Tim Hunter who, among other credits, had directed the chilling teen drug and murder movie *River's Edge*, which starred Keanu Reeves and one of Jason Priestley's idols, Dennis Hopper.

It was a creative team from amazingly diverse backgrounds, but one thing was certain: the results would be different *and* interesting!

At this early point in its history, the show was going to be called *The Class of Beverly Hills*, but that didn't really say what the show was all about. Just calling it *Beverly Hills* didn't get anyone revved up either: that made the show sound too much like a stodgy old *Dallas* or *Knot's Landing*, which it definitely was *not*.

Then, during a meeting, someone suggested just using the Beverly Hills zip code, *90210*. That sounded fresh, and everyone went along with it. (That is, until shortly before the show went on the air. They began to wonder if people would *get* what the numbers meant, or if maybe it was a tad *too* cool. Though we fans call the show *90210* today, it finally premiered as *Beverly Hills, 90210*.)

But the title wasn't the only problem.

It was now late in the spring of 1990, and Fox wanted the show to debut on October 4. That meant it had to start shooting six weeks before that date, in August, so there'd be time to edit the film, score the music, and do other "post-production" chores. *That* meant they had to start casting *pronto*.

As we said before, Hollywood is a town full of young actors who want to be stars. So when Fox held an open call for the show—which meant that anyone could try out, even people without agents or experience—the flood of young people was more like a tidal wave. The studio was overrun with starry-eyed hopefuls!

Photos were collected by the producers and their assistants, and notes were made on the back. They wrote down phone numbers. They hoped they'd find *someone* to fill the bill.

For the most part, they were incredibly successful. They found experienced actresses for all of the girls' parts, and experienced actors to play most of the boys.

Yet, despite the hundreds of young men who tried out for Brandon, no one seemed to be just right for the part. No one had that special combination of innocence and sexiness that was so important to the character. (Dylan McKay still hadn't been created at this point.)

The producers started calling back some of the applicants, and also began auditioning actors in New York and Chicago.

The results? Zippo.

Months dragged on. Shooting was scheduled to start in less than a week and, understandably, the producers were beginning to get a little *panicky*. They narrowed the choice for Brandon down to a few *good* actors . . . but they still hadn't seen a *perfect* one. And since the success of the show would depend heavily on the charisma of the leading man, they were getting pretty depressed.

Finally, with shooting set to begin in less than a week, they had to make a choice. And they were about to award the part to another actor when, fortunately for them (and us!), a miracle occurred.

Chapter 15

Sister Kate had just been canceled. Technically, Jason Priestly was free to try out for other parts.

But before actors can audition for other shows or movies, they have to be released, officially, from their obligations to the show they were just on. There's always the slim chance that the network will change its mind at the last minute and suddenly order more episodes. (Just ask actor Pierce Brosnan about that. He was all set to be the movies' new James Bond when (boo!) NBC changed its mind about cancelling his show *Remington Steele* and ordered six more episodes. Or ask Tom Selleck, who was picked to play Indiana Jones in *Raiders of the Lost Ark* when CBS decided to buy his show *Magnum, P.I.*!)

Jason Priestley finally got his release from *Sister Kate* a little over a week before *Beverly Hills, 90210* was set to start shooting. Amazing as it seems, just eight days before he would become Brandon Walsh, Jason had never even *heard* of the character.

What's even more amazing is that when his agent called and told him about the part, Jason wasn't even sure it was worth trying out for!

No, he wasn't being picky. He didn't want to get his hopes up and have them dashed. The show was set to go before the cameras in seven measly days: he knew that people in Hollywood don't tend to make casting decisions of that magnitude that fast!

Besides, his hair was over-the-collar longish from *Sister Kate*, and there wouldn't be time to get a haircut to try out for clean-cut Brandon.

But Jason's agent assured him that this audition would be a *little* different from the ones he was used to in that the people at Fox had *asked* to see him. *Sister Kate* had been filmed at the Fox studio, and someone there realized that Jason was suddenly available and just might be right for the part.

The agent convinced Jason that he had nothing to lose, so, rather than dwelling on it, the actor hopped on his bike and went over to the studio to audition.

"I got the script and went in at the very last minute." He laughs. "My first audition was on Thursday and I went to the network on Friday (a call-back so the producers could see him), and I started on Monday. It was *that* last minute."

(Oh, yeah . . . he *did* find time that weekend to get a haircut!)

Was he excited when he heard he'd gotten the part?

No. When his agent called him on Friday night, he was *ecstatic!* Jason liked the idea of doing a show that dealt with important teen issues, and he *loved* the idea of working with Tim Hunter and the other creative people involved . . . which, as it turned out, would include his pal Melman.

He also liked the cast members (one of whom he had already worked with . . . but we're not telling *who*, just yet) and knew he would hit it off with them.

And what, incidentally, did Aaron Spelling think of his find? Mr. Spelling, who has seen big stars come and go, has nothing but oodles of praise for Jason.

After a few episodes had been filmed, Mr. Spelling said, "Jason has been our quarterback, keeping everybody on an even keel. I think Jason is the date that every girl would like to have. He's very attractive, he's sensitive, and he seems safe."

Mr. Spelling chuckles and adds, "That's why we brought in Luke Perry, because we thought we needed a character who was a little more off-center, who was a little James Dean."

Dean, of course, was the 1950s superstar movie rebel and Perry look-alike who was killed in a car crash too soon after his brilliant career had begun.

It had been a heckuva a week for Jason: losing one show and being depressed, getting another show and being elated. He'd always known that acting was going to have its ups and downs, but he never imagined that they'd be like this!

Even so, he'd have been shocked to learn that there were even bigger highs and some surprising lows just ahead.

Chapter 16

As we mentioned before, the producers had a much easier time finding actors to play the other characters in the show. And talk about *experience*: almost every member of the cast has more credentials than Beverly Hills has BMWs!

For the important part of Brenda, they signed vivacious young actress Shannen Maria Doherty. The twenty-year-old, five-foot three-inch native of Memphis, Tennessee, had played Jenny Wilder on the last season (1982–1983) of *Little House on the Prairie*, had starred as fifteen-year-old Kris Witherspoon in the series *Our House*, which ran on NBC from 1986 to 1988, and had also costarred in the critically acclaimed theatrical film *Heathers*, with Winona Ryder.

For her friend Kelly, they picked nineteen-year-old, five-foot five-inch Jennie Garth, who had recently moved to Los Angeles from Phoenix, Arizona (after spending most of her life in rural Champaign, Illinois, where she grew up on a farm).

Nineteen-year-old Jennie had made her acting debut in the TV movie *A Brand New Life* with Barbara Eden (of *I Dream of Jeannie* fame) and after that costarred in—guess what?—*Teen Angel Returns*!

(Wouldn't you think she'd have *told* the producers about Jason when *Sister Kate* was canned and they were tearing their hair out, looking for Brandon? She admits that she *should* have, and says she has no idea why it didn't occur to her . . . though she was delighted when Jason got the part.) Jennie had also made *Just Perfect* for the Disney Channel, and appeared in *Growing Pains*.

To play the intellectual Andrea, the producers hired another Phoenix native, five-foot one-inch Gabrielle Carteris. (Even though she had come to audition for the part of Brenda! And by the way—guess who *else* originally came in and tried out for a different part than the one he got? Read on . . .)

A former ballet dancer, Gabrielle had appeared in a few after school specials, the acclaimed *What If I'm Gay?, Seasonal Differences,* and *Just Between Friends*, and also had a recurring role in the soap opera *Another World* (with another of her *Beverly Hills, 90210* costars . . . though we're not telling you *who*, yet) and a part in the movie *Jacknife* with Robert DeNiro. Not bad! At thirty, she's the oldest "teen" member of the cast.

Tori Spelling was cast as Donna, and yep—she's that teenaged daughter of the Aaron Spelling we were talking about earlier. Thing is, Tori tried out for the part without telling her father. And to make sure she wasn't hired just *because* of who she was (would *you* like to be the casting agent who had to tell a powerful producer that his daughter was a crumola actress?), Tori auditioned for the role under a fake name!

An incredibly bashful young girl, Tori says she originally became an actress *not* because her dad was in the business, but because it "was the only way to overcome my terrible shyness. It forced me to speak to people and to stand up for myself."

Tori began her career at the age of six, appearing in an episode of the TV series *Vegas*. Since then, her credentials have included roles in the TV movie *The Three Kings*, with Lou Diamond Phillips, and—an ironic hint of things to come!—in the theatrical movie *Troop Beverly Hills*.

For the show's angelic mom, the producers selected forty-two-year-old Carol Potter, a veteran of oodles of stage plays, TV movies, and the short-lived series *Today's F.B.I.*

Considering the problems they had casting Brandon, finding an actress to play Cindy was a breeze: according to Tony Shepherd, one of the folks in charge of the casting, "She's the first person we saw, and everybody just went 'Wow!' She reacts right from the gut."

Wow indeed!

On the male side . . .

For David, the producers turned to Brian Austin Green, who had just graduated from high school that June and was able to capture the essence of an *annoying student*. Professionally, he had played Brian Cunningham on *Knot's Landing*, and had also appeared in such shows as *Highway to Heaven* and *The New Leave It To Beaver*, as well as in the recent movie *Kickboxer II*.

Ian Ziering—who pronounces his first name *Eye-an, not Ee*-an—has been an actor since the age of twelve, and holds a college degree in dramatic arts. He made his acting debut in the movie *Endless Love* starring Brooke Shields, and spent two-and-a-half years playing Cameron Stewart on the daytime soap opera *The Guiding Light*.

He also had roles on the soaps *Love of Life* and *The Doctors* before moving to Beverly Hills and prime time as Steve Sanders.

(To tell the truth, Ziering says he misses those soap opera days more than a little. He feels that those shows taught him to be a strong, instinctive actor.)

"A lot of people try to put down daytime dramas," he says, "dismiss them as 'soap operas.' But there's a lot of good writing, good acting, and hard work involved in turning out all that drama, day after day, with so little opportunity for preparation or rehearsal."

And here's a little coincidence for you. On *The Guiding Light*, one of Ziering's costars was hunky John Wesley Shipp, an actor who hit the big time the same year as Ziering, playing TV's *The Flash*. Now that *The Flash* has zoomed off to the TV graveyard, don't be surprised if Shipp does a guest spot on his old costar's show!

There's *another*, even neater coincidence about Ian's soap opera career . . . but you'll learn more about that in a little while!)

Sixteen-year-old Douglas Emerson, an actor since the age of four when he starred in a candy commercial, was picked to play Scott. Among his zillion or so credits are guest spots on the TV series *The Wonder Years, Night Court, Highway to Heaven*, and the soap opera *General Hospital*.

On the big screen, Douglas has appeared in the remake of *The Blob*, in *Police Academy*, and in writer Steve Burkow's terrif wrestling flick, *Body Slam*.

The part of dad Jim went to James Eckhouse, an actor who was a physics and biology major at that International House of Eggheads, MIT in Cambridge, Massachusetts. However, after two years, he switched to acting and went to the famed Julliard School.

After graduating, Eckhouse landed one role after another in shows like *Matlock* and *thirtysomething*, and in movies such as *Cocktail* and *Defending Your Life*.

As for the latecoming but key role of Dylan McKay, that was another incredibly important piece of casting.

The producers needed someone who could convincingly embody the dark side of life, just as Brandon represented the light. And just as good Brandon actors weren't plentiful, good Dylans were as rare as fresh fish in Moscow.

Luckily, not only did the producers score their second major home run, but it didn't take as many turns at bat to do it!

Chapter 17

Unlike Jason Priestley, who literally fell into the part of Brandon, Luke Perry worked long and hard to get the role of Dylan McKay—longer and harder than any cast member worked to get their part, and longer and harder than he ever worked for *anything* in his career!

When Luke's agent told him that there was going to be an open call for all of the parts on *Beverly Hills, 90210*—get this!—Luke decided to go and try out for the role of Steve Sanders!

What! you say. *Steve Sanders?* Lanky Luke isn't anything like big, muscular Steve!

True, but remember: there *was* no Dylan KcKay when auditions were first held.

So why did Luke bother auditioning? Because he wasn't up for any other roles at the time, and apart from actually landing a movie or TV show, the most important thing in Hollywood is to be *seen*, whenever and wherever you can. You never know when another part will come up, and some producer or casting agent will remember your face or the way you delivered a line or the way you walked into the room. (Just like the folks at Fox remembered Jason from *Sister Kate*.)

So, in his quiet, laid-back way, Luke says that, yes, "I knew going in I wasn't right for him [Steve]." And he wasn't surprised when "it didn't go so well. I knew I wasn't physically right for him, and it didn't strike me as a role that I would be able to find a lot in." (Which, incidentally, is one reason he respects Ian Ziering so very much. Luke says with heartfelt admiration, "It's really a credit to Ian because he *has* found so much to do with the character.")

But he went to be *seen*. And good thing he did, too.

After failing to make an impression as Steve, Luke went back to the day job he held, and also continued auditioning for other parts.

Then, in July, he got a call from his agent saying that a new character had been added to the *Beverly Hills, 90210* roster, one that the agent didn't think Luke would have any trouble playing. (And was *that* the understatement of the year, or what?) The Fox team had remembered Luke from his failed Steve Sanders audition, and wanted to see him again.

Luke got an appointment with the casting people, and had to tell his boss "huge lies" to get out of work so he could go to the audition.

Walking into the casting room, Luke was handed some photocopied pages of script featuring Dylan's dialogue. He had a few minutes to study it, then went in to see Tony Shepherd and his people.

This time, the casting folks were *ultra*-impressed at how right Luke seemed for this part, and asked him to come back and read for them again.

He did.

Then they asked him to come in and read again.

He did.

Then again.

He did.

The twenty-four-year-old actor went in four times, then went *back* to read for Aaron Spelling himself. After *that* meeting—which Luke says was nerve-wracking, because Mr. Spelling is a living legend—the actor was asked to come to the studio for a *sixth* audition, this time for the executives at Fox.

He did, and that night, the phone rang in his Los Angeles apartment.

It was his agent. Luke's heart was drumming like a beaver's tail. He waited, palms sweating as he listened to the words he wanted to hear:

"You got the part!"

"No kidding!" he said, breaking into a wide, very un-Dylan-like smile.

Of all the actors working on *Beverly Hills, 90210*, it's likely that Luke Perry cherishes his good fortune the most.

Later, when he's standing in the warehouse parking lot, he looks around and says, "I used to *make* parking lots. The only thing I know how to do besides act is physical labor. I was a paver, I was a cook, I drove people around in their Mercedes, I worked in a video store, I sold shoes, I worked in a hotel, made a lot of beds myself."

Luke's had a tougher life than most, and he's certainly come farther from his roots than anyone but farm girl Jennie Garth.

But Luke is unique in other ways, too. He is without a doubt the most serious of the young actors (even more so than *tres* serious Jason): he gets *completely* into every part he plays so thoroughly that . . .

Well, you'll read in a while what kind of strange things can happen to a guy so devoted to his craft.

Perhaps what separates Luke from the other actors more than anything, though, is that most of his costars are nothing like the characters they play. But Luke and Dylan have a great deal in common.

With the kind of emotion that makes you want to pat his back and tell him everything's going to be all right, he says, "There are certain situations in Dylan's life that hook me . . . things I find a little close to home."

It's those dramatic similarities between Luke and Dylan that come across on TV, and that make both the actor and the character he plays so fascinating.

As you read his story, try to imagine the occasional smile, the soft voice, sometimes sad, and the strength and character in his eyes as he talks about his life . . .

Chapter 18

Luke Perry was born on October 11, 1964, in Mansfield, Ohio, but was raised in Fredericktown, a small place twenty miles away and far from the major cities of Cleveland and Cincinnati.

A farm boy, Luke describes himself and his family as "good, hardworking." When he was young, he took care of the "cows, sheep, roosters, the whole thing. And I worked pitching hay, all that stuff."

Luke didn't come from a show business family. In fact, the only person in his family who had anything to do with the arts was a favorite uncle of his, who was a musician when he was younger.

Luke smiles as he remembers. "I do have very vivid memories of being a child watching him on-stage and him calling me up to sing a couple of songs with his band."

And what songs did the young boy get up and sing? Elevator music? Frank Sinatra songs? Broadway ditties? Not *this* dude!

He says, "I sang 'Hotel California' by the Eagles." The man was cool, even at the age of twelve!

But really good memories like that are rare for Luke, who says, "To say that my childhood was idyllic would not be true. We certainly had our rough times."

When Luke was just six years old, he suffered through a very Dylan-like experience: his parents were divorced.

69

Now, he's the first to tell you he's not *alone* in suffering that: "If you asked eighty percent of the people in the United States, right now," he says, "they would have the same story." But it still had a big impact on the boy.

"My relationship with my father was very strained," he says. "It certainly opened my eyes to things early on in life."

Such as? He says he learned that "parents are not perfect people in general, and everyone can make a mistake."

It also taught him not to look to other people to *give* him happiness, but to search within himself to find it. "You have got to be happy first and then share it with someone else," he believes, "as opposed to really needing something so bad from someone else."

Pretty heavy thoughts for a six-year-old, but Luke has always been *very* observant, very thoughtful, and very aware. He says he's also very lucky to have had the support of a loving brother, Tom, who is three years older, and a sister Amy, who is three years younger than Luke. (He also has a much younger stepsister, Emily, who is fourteen.)

When Luke's mother was remarried to a construction worker, the family moved frequently to go where the jobs were. Yet, even when they ended up in big cities—which was most of the time—Luke never lost the small town qualities he grew up with: kindness, willingness to work hard, and a deep, deep appreciation for anything he earned.

Like many kids, Luke wasn't sure what he wanted to do when he graduated from school. He enjoyed being outdoors, but couldn't see himself becoming a forest ranger or anything like that, and he loved all kinds of animals, though he didn't want to go back to the farm or work as a veterinarian (he doesn't like seeing animals in pain) or in a pet shop (he doesn't like seeing them caged, either).

Luke also loved *danger*, but though he rode a motorcycle, he couldn't see himself becoming a professional stuntman or a daredevil like his hero, thrill-seeker Evel Knievel. (Luke used to have posters of the action star tacked to his bedroom wall.)

Two things that interested him greatly and made a lot more sense as careers the older he got: music and acting.

Musically, Luke loved 1950s rock and roll and opera (yes . . . *opera!*), though he never really wanted to become a singer. He wasn't sure he had the voice for it, and he didn't know if he'd be that good on the guitar or drums. (What is he, *kidding?* With his looks, people would've paid to hear Luke play a toy piano!)

But TV was another matter. Luke was a big fan of action shows, especially *Starsky & Hutch* (which, ironically, was produced by Aaron Spelling) and *The Rockford Files*. And of course he loved movies on TV, especially adventure movies.

"I used to watch movies all the time," he confesses. "The afternoon movie, the late movie, you name it."

In fact, it was a movie he saw on TV when he was twelve years old, a movie made in 1967, that changed his life. It became his number one favorite movie and edged him toward becoming an actor—an ambition that built up steam over the years. (Especially whenever he saw this film!)

The movie was *Cool Hand Luke* and it starred Paul Newman—an actor who, in the 1950s and early 1960s, was considered a rebellious kinda guy, just like Luke is today.

Cool Hand Luke was about the kind of men who live in prison. Newman played a sarcastic but charming

71

loner (sound familiar?) who steals not just to survive, but because he hates those in authority and wants to do anything he can to assert his *own* authority. Even in jail, he rejects the friendship of other prisoners at first—until his attitude and individualism win their respect.

However, the film's sad but strangely heroic star wasn't the only thing about the movie that attracted Luke Perry. Guess what did?

Luke laughs. "I saw my *name* on TV! That was the best. I'd never even seen it in *writing* before! I must've watched that movie fifty times!"

The other movie that really blew Luke away was the big, award-winning 1962 epic *Lawrence of Arabia*. Though the idea of war has never thrilled Luke (How could it? Brother Tom is in the United States Navy!), he could relate to Lawrence, a British soldier who defied his superiors to help the people of a foreign land fight for their freedom. He was a *major* antiauthority figure, and Luke grooved on that.

The funny thing is, despite the fact that Luke was attracted to movies and TV shows about righteous rebel dudes, he himself was *not* the kind of guy to attack authority figures.

He grins and says that he may have *wanted* to be a little rebellious, but "I held back on what I thought sometimes" out of respect for his teachers. Also, he was greatly concerned about how it would affect his family if he were ever caught doing something wrong. It would have upset him greatly to have caused *them* any heartache.

By the time he reached high school, Luke was doing any and all the acting he could.

Oh, he played baseball and tennis on the school teams in order to stay in shape and be with his friends. But even when it came to athletics, the most fun he

An impish smile from the hunkiest rebel in Beverly Hills,
Luke Perry. *Photo: Shooting Star.*

The killer eyes tell you why Luke is going to be one of the decade's biggest stars. *Photo: Shooting Star.*

Luke Perry's James Dean look: remote, rebellious, and totally adorable! *Photo: Shooting Star.*

Luke seems to be wondering whether to go with the plaid jacket or strip down to his famous tee. (Either way's cool by us, Luke!) *Photo: Shooting Star.*

"Yeah, we're gonna lick *Cheers* this season!" Jason seems to be saying as he shoves his hands in his pockets and puts on a defiant expression. *Photo: Shooting Star.*

The face that helped make Luke Perry an idol to millions: the furrowed brow, sexy sunken cheeks, and stylish earring. *Photo: Shooting Star.*

Unshaven, his brow lowered in thought, Jason shows us his serious side. *Photo: Shooting Star.*

Luke the duke looking outrageous — the man in plaid with those dynamite dagger 'burns. *Photo: Shooting Star.*

The term "blazer" takes on a new meaning when it's worn by one of the heroes of Beverly Hills. *Photo: Shooting Star.*

Jason trying a slicked-back look. The guy just doesn't know *how* to take a bad picture! *Photo: Shooting Star.*

A weekend stubble and eyes that'll turn your heart to a puddle: the power of Jason Priestley. *Photo: Shooting Star.*

Luke makes a fast getaway from a mall. (How close did he come to getting mauled? See inside.) *Photo: Star File.*

Jason Priestley — the vulnerable, sensitive guy every teenage girl would love to date! *Photo: Shooting Star.*

ever had, he says, was playing his school's mascot, Freddy the Bird.

"It was fun," he recalls. "I rode into football games on a helicopter and did wheelies on my dirt bike."

However, while that was all a blast and very exciting, Luke was pretty disappointed in what was *really* important to him: the school's drama department. In a word, it was ill.

"I was in the theater program," he says, but for four years "we did the same three plays over and over again!" Though he cherished his time on the stage, he would have loved to learn new lines and try his hand at other parts!

But the failings of his high school drama department were a relatively small problem. When he was still a teenager, Luke realized that he had an even bigger problem: in order to become a professional actor, he couldn't continue living in Ohio.

"I had big ambitions," he says, "and living in a small town and not being able to do anything about my goals was very frustrating."

Which isn't to say that Luke *resents* his small town beginnings. Quite the contrary. He says today, "I have a feeling that if I had grown up in L.A. or New York City, I might be a lot different, and I wouldn't have liked that." He adds, "You learn valuable things about people when you live in the country."

He stops talking for a moment, folds his hands, looks deep inside of himself and says from the heart, "The beautiful part about living in a small town is that you really develop a good sense of who *you* really are."

So if you've ever wondered why and how Luke hasn't been changed by his recent hyper-achievements . . . there's the reason. His good heart and good self-image were solidly set before he headed to Tinseltown.

Anyway . . .

Luke knew that he had to go to New York or Los Angeles to act, and he also felt it would be a good idea to get himself some acting lessons. And L.A. or New York were the only places he could do that, too.

Since there was no one he could *ask* about how he should go about becoming an actor, he went to the library and read biographies about his favorite actors to see how *they* had made it. And all of them—Paul Newman and Marlon Brando in particular—got their starts studying and doing stage work in New York.

But he knew that they'd grown up in a different era, when there was a *lot* of stage work available and live TV was just beginning to happen. Today, it would be harder to get work there, since most of the TV shows and even the soap operas were being shot in Los Angeles.

Besides, Newman and Brando both eventually went to Hollywood, because that's where the movies were being made, where the really great parts were. So did the other actor whose work Luke admired, an actor to whom he would one day be compared over and over.

That actor personified the young rebel, the Hollywood bad boy—James Dean.

So after weighing the pros and cons, Luke decided that Hollywood it would be.

Chapter 19

With the support and encouragement of his family, and a Tupperware container filled with his mom's cooking (something he knew he'd miss terribly when he left home), Luke headed west just as soon as he finished high school.

His traveling companion was a pet, a small farm-bred pig named Jerry Lee (after Luke's favorite rock and roller, 1950s star Jerry Lee Lewis).

Jerry Lee was not only a good friend—he never talked back, never snorted a discouraging word—but he was a constant reminder of the love that waited for Luke back in Ohio. Come what may, success or failure, he'd always have the love and support of the family he'd grown up with on the farm. The pig was (and remains) a very important part of Luke's life!

(Luke's pet dog, Tuck, stayed with the folks in Ohio.)

Luke had money he'd saved from working part-time jobs for the last three years, and he had his goals and ambitions—but that, the pig, and the clothes in his duffel bag (Luke's bag, not the pig's) were it.

Arriving in Los Angeles, Luke took a super-small apartment, got a part-time job (and then another, and another, and another after that, leaving when he would get fired after missing work to go on auditions), and visited several acting teachers to ask if he could study with them.

Several of them who auditioned the young man

thought he had real potential, and one was happy to take him on as a student.

As soon as he started taking lessons, Luke also started going on auditions. He felt that even though he had no professional experience, he had nothing to lose by trying—and he wanted the experience of being handed lines, learning them in a hurry, and trying to make an impression on casting agents.

What he discovered was that these people saw *dozens* of aspiring actors every day, and each actor had only five minutes *tops* to make a favorable impression on them.

It was a challenge, to be sure, and like Jason Priestley he realized he'd not only have to be good to get parts, but lucky as well.

But that was fine with him. Luke was in no rush to get rich or famous. He wasn't *used* to being rich anyway: all he wanted to do was to sharpen his talents. Even today, he says that getting parts is not as important to him as getting better at what he does.

"A person can never stop improving their craft," he believes. "Even though I'm working on a series, I'm still taking acting classes."

And though his first months in Hollywood were very lean ones, he never lost even a *sliver* of his incredible courage or optimism.

Part of this was due to his own confidence and determination to succeed. Part of it was due to his family and friends, who he knew were pulling for him. Even today, he says, "Some of the best friends I've *ever* made come from Ohio," and he still calls them "every other day, just to talk."

However, *part* of it was due to the fact that for Luke, doing quality work is more important than being busy or making a lot of money. Even today, when he has an income higher than his show's zip code, he says, "I *never* want to be a rich person in Beverly Hills, someone who is so wealthy it completely changes the person that they are.

"That is a dangerous place to be, and something that I certainly would try to avoid."

He adds, "I don't prize possessions. I prize people. My friends are the most valuable things in my life."

Three cheers for Luke!

However, don't think that *sometimes* the pressure of auditions didn't get to Luke. He wouldn't be human if *nothing* bothered him. Quite often, there were parts he wanted very badly and didn't get . . . and that would be enough to disappoint *anyone*.

When that happened, he would pull a Jason Priestley (though he was doing it three years before the Jay-man): he'd go out to the lonely, desolate Death Valley and ride his dirt bike around the desert.

Today, even though he could afford to travel first class to any place on the planet, that hot, dry, deserted place remains Luke Perry's favorite vacation spot.

Or else, for relaxation, he'd find an empty parking lot somewhere and take his bike apart. He says that one of the most calming things in the world to him is to "take things apart to see how they work," though he says he has even more fun "putting stuff back together."

As with Jason, these hobbies helped him to clear his head, remind himself that it was only *one* part he'd missed, that there would be other roles. At least he was doing what he wanted to in life, and that was something to be *very* thankful for.

Back in his apartment, as a kind of "calendar" of progress, Luke did something he'd once seen in the movie *Jason and the Argonauts*. In the film, a member of the crew keeps track of how many days they've been at sea by making marks on the deck of the ship.

When he arrived in L.A., Luke decided to put a piece of paper on the refrigerator and make marks on it, one for every audition he went to before he got a job.

77

After a year and a half, there were 216 lines on the piece of paper! He had gone to that many auditions without getting work . . . and, impossible as it is to believe, without getting completely discouraged.

Let this be a lesson to all aspiring actors: you've *got* to hold on! Because audition number 217 was about to bring about a change in the young man's fortunes!

Chapter 20

Like Jason and most every other young actor just starting out, Luke was always auditioning for everything he could, from theatrical movies to TV movies, from prime-time series to soap operas, from TV commercials to stage plays.

Since soap operas are on every weekday, and there are so many supporting characters who come and go each week, those were what he ended up auditioning for the most. Like Ian, he felt that a soap opera would be a great training ground.

On several occasions, West Coast representatives of New York soap operas were impressed with Luke (which doesn't exactly put them in the genius class, does it?) and had him fly east to see their bosses.

Unfortunately, he never got any of those parts, though he remembers that once, "I went to New York to test for a part and Ian [Ziering] was there too! We were competing against each other for the same part.

"And I thought, 'What is he, greedy? He already *has* a job [on *Guiding Light*] and he wants *two*?'" That really blew Luke's mind.

But in talking to Ian, Luke learned that the young actor was anything *but* greedy. He was trying to grow. He didn't have much to do on *Guiding Light*, so he wanted to get a second part so he'd keep busy and get experience.

(Ian didn't get the part they were trying out for either. But the *Guiding Light* producers were afraid of losing him, so they made his part bigger.)

As it turns out, Luke's 217th audition was for a soap opera: for the part of Ned Bates on *Loving*, which was taped at the ABC studios in New York. His first interview was in Southern California, and they liked him there; so, once again, Luke was put on a plane and sent east for further auditions.

This time, though, his trip to the Big Apple bore fruit: the casting people loved him, and he got his first professional acting job.

Luke was watching TV in his hotel room when he got the word from his agent. He remembers snapping up the phone even before the first ring was finished, half-expecting it to be his mother calling to see if he'd gotten any feedback from the audition. Boy, was *he* surprised when it was his agent, telling him that the part was his.

After doing a little dance around the room, Luke's first call was (did you guess?) to his mother back in Ohio.

She was thrilled to tears for her son, and Luke admits that he was also thrilled for himself: unlike so many young people who go into acting with high hopes that are eventually dashed, the determined young man was *finally* going to begin earning a living as an actor.

The very next morning, Luke got himself an apartment in New York, then made a quick trip back to L.A. to say good-bye to a few pals, pick up his belongings, and break the news to Jerry Lee. Then it was back to New York to start working on the show.

Though Luke admits he "never dug" the name of his character, he loved the part.

He loved the hot studio lights.

He loved the pressure of having to learn newly written pages that were thrust at him just minutes before the taping was to start . . . that, on top of up to *sixty* pages of script he'd already be studying *each and every day*!

He loved the feeling of belonging to a family of actors, of having somewhere to go to do what he enjoyed doing.

He loved getting a couple of fan letters a week, answering them personally and thoughtfully, giving his autograph to fans waiting outside the studio, often in the rain.

He loved knowing that his work was touching people in television land. Acting is something that people do for themselves, but Luke was coming to understand just how much you could give to others by doing it . . . just like Paul Newman's Cool Hand Luke had given so much to him!

He loved being asked to make personal appearances on behalf of various charities (where he often ran into Ian Ziering). It was a chance for him to give something back to the viewers who had helped him to realize his goal.

And he also loved being in New York. Though he never lost the small town values he had—helping people who seemed lost, reaching into his pocket and giving money to those who needed it, assisting an elderly person crossing the street or hailing a cab for them— he found himself thriving on the movement of the big city, on the many, many museums, on the Broadway plays and movies and just hanging out with other actors.

He often went down to famous Greenwich Village and ate in little cafés, listened to artists talking with other artists, actors with actors, dancers with dancers. He soaked up the life and beat of the great metropolis.

It was a tremendously educational time in Luke's life. And though he had never minded the honest work he'd been doing back in Los Angeles to put food on the table, he had to admit that playing Ned sure beat flipping burger meat!

While he was working, Luke also took advantage of the many acting teachers available to him in New York, studying at some of the very same places where Paul Newman and Marlon Brando had studied.

He says it's interesting: he *thought* he was a good actor before he came to New York. But after working on *Loving* and studying with other teachers—especially the legendary acting coaches Bobby Lewis and Marcia Jean Kurtz—he realized how very much he still had to learn!

This supremely levelheaded star has *never* wondered what would have happened to his career if he'd come to New York first instead of heading to California. Luke isn't the kind of guy who plays "what if" or cries over mistakes. He feels that he's learned something from *everything* he's done, whether it furthered his career or not.)

After a year on *Loving*, Luke was looking to stretch his acting muscles a little, and tried out for and won an even larger part, playing Kenny on the soap opera *Another World*, which was also being taped in New York.

(Luke's costar on the show was Joe Morton, who *also* went on to prime-time fame as a star of *Equal Justice*, and then on to gory glory as the doomed scientist in the film *Terminator 2*.

And, of course, remember who else was on this show? None other than Gabrielle Carteris. As the saying goes, *It's a small world . . .*)

In addition to having more lines, the new job paid Luke more money . . . which, though it wasn't the *most* important thing in his life, allowed him to save for the future, when jobs might not be so plentiful.

Luke enjoyed the new show just as much as the

previous one, and there was something *else* he dis-covered that was great about working in television. You're not only seen by viewers, but also by prospective employers.

In Luke's case, while he was on *Another World*, he was spotted by a producer who wanted to make a low-budget film called *Terminal Bliss*. Luke was called in to audition, and he was hired for the leading role as John.

The movie was not successful, though it did lead to his second film: *Scorchers*, directed by acting teacher David Beard and also starring Faye Dunaway and James Earl Jones (the voice of Darth Vader in the *Star Wars* films).

Scorchers—which is scheduled for release at the end of this year—is a film of which Luke is very proud. However, he says that even if it ends up being a stinker, he got what he *really* wanted out of it: the chance to act with a pair of giants in the profession.

Like Jason when he worked with the cast of *The Boy Who Could Fly*, Luke got to see how truly classy profes-sionals conducted themselves on a motion picture set. James Earl Jones in particular made a big impression on him, and he also learned a lot watching the great man act.

In order to make these films, Luke had been forced to leave *Another World* and return to California. It's always a tough decision for an actor, whether to leave the security of a show to take a movie, or whether to stay and collect a paycheck. For Luke, though, there was never any question: he went where there was knowledge to be gained.

But now, there he was, late in 1989, back in Hollywood with only a little money saved up (New York is an even more expensive place to live than Los Angeles!) and with some good but not powerhouse credentials.

Things were almost exactly like they were nearly two years before when Luke had first headed to New York. He had to start auditioning all over again—for soap operas, movies, TV shows, and commercials—though he *did* have the advantage of bringing a little more experience to his tryouts. There was a newfound confidence behind that ever-cool exterior: he knew it, and casting agents sensed it.

Though Luke was working a part-time day job to help pay the bills, he felt sure it wouldn't be long before good opportunities opened up for him. Patience, he had learned, was an important part of an acting career!

And that was the way things were when he went to audition for the part of Steve on *Beverly Hills, 90210* . . .

Chapter 21

You're back on the set, having been entranced watching a full morning of shooting . . .

The scene between Dylan and Brenda, which they'd been rehearsing, has now been shot—or, as they say in the biz, is in the can.

Several other scenes also have been finished, involving Shannen and Jason, and their characters' preparations for the trip. Now it's time to break for lunch.

As everyone leaves, you discover that being on the set of *Beverly Hills, 90210* can be much worse than having a sweet tooth in a candy shop: you watch as the *ultimate* young superstars go off in different directions, to their respective trailers, and you can only follow one of them at a time.

Who will it be?

Jason is still casually flipping the hat onto his head, obviously entertained by the nifty move, and looking smooth and very approachable. Luke is walking away more slowly, those wide shoulders swaying slowly from side to side as he pores over his script.

You're dying to know about Jason's big secret, the one he didn't get to answer before, but you're also seriously in love with Luke and you want to hang with him for a while, too, find out more about the silent, brooding star.

Jason or Luke—*what a choice!*

Fortunately, Shannen unwittingly makes the decision for you!

When the actress leaves the set, she hurries to catch up with Jason, to discuss a private matter with him. (Something hot? Well . . . sort of. You later learn that the two of them are going to the Emmy awards together, and need to make plans. You wonder if Luke has a date—and, after asking around later, find out that he does. Like that's a surprise!)

But right now, at least, Luke is free, and you head after him as he disappears through that big open garage-like door.

Luke's small dressing room is accessible from the outside, and he's heading toward it. The dressing room is like all the others in the converted warehouse: small, private, and functional.

You catch up to him as he's about to enter, and though he's probably starving and would really rather eat his lunch than talk, he graciously invites you in, standing back so you can enter first.

You hurry in and sit on the small couch that is tucked against one wall; he sits in a chair across from you, hunched forward. You wonder if he notices that your hands are shaking—trembling like a terrier tied to a tree at a wiener roast!

He asks if you're having a good time.

Uhhhh, no, you think. I'd rather be on the set of *The CBS Evening News*.

You tell him *of course* you're having a good time— trying to be blasé about it, but failing when your voice cracks.

He smiles as you swallow hard and tell him—truthfully—that of all the sets you've visited over the years, this one is the most exciting.

Now it's Luke who seems a little embarrassed, but he thanks you just the same. He reaches around to the mini-refrigerator nearby and offers you a bottle of mineral water. You accept it because your mouth is drier than a charred burger. He rubs the little green bottle against his jeans to wipe away the sweat, and hands it to you (the bottle, not the jeans), then takes one for himself.

Water, it turns out, is Luke's favorite drink. He says it totally cleanses the body and really rejuvenates him.

And what's his favorite food? you ask.

Mexican. Also steak and potatoes, though he says he likes to cook them himself and fix them in different and interesting ways.

What about his favorite color?

He thinks for a moment, then answers, "All of them."

"Really?" you ask, surprised.

Really, he says. He explains that if he sees something beautiful, whether it's a person or a flower or a '63 Porsche convertible, then to him, the color of that thing is also beautiful.

You're impressed by his sensitivity, which doesn't often have a chance to come through when he's playing Dylan. And though you'd like to ask his opinions about so many things, you know your time here is limited. So . . .

You take a sip of mineral water and think. Obviously, there are a couple of *personal* questions you'd like to have answered, and you decide to ask those last, starting with some of the *less* personal ones . . .

Chapter 22

You ask lean, mean Luke how much he weighs.

He pats the flat tum and says it varies. When he's working hard, he actually *forgets* to eat sometimes. Usually, though, he tips the scales at between 135 and 140 pounds.

Where does he live?

"In Hollywood," he says. "Got a two-bedroom house."

Does Jerry Lee like it?

"A *lot*." Luke smiles. "I have a big yard for him and he's a great pet."

What does Luke drive when he's not dirt-biking it?

"Just got a new truck," he says proudly. "Four-wheel drive—really cool."

You know about his favorite old movies; are there any recent movies that really knocked him out?

You're not surprised by his answer: *Great Balls of Fire*, the biopic starring Dennis Quaid as Luke's favorite rocker, Jerry Lee Lewis.

Does he wish *he* had played the part?

He gives you an *Are you kidding?* look. Luke thinks Dennis Quaid did a great job, but he'd have killed to have that part!

Favorite TV show?

Jeopardy!, he says. He likes learning things.

What's the *nuttiest* thing he's ever done?

He purses his lips, then says he'll tell you—but he wants you to understand that he has always enjoyed the *thrill* of life. He says that's why he goes bungee jumping whenever he can—leaping off high places like bridges and cliffs, stopping before he *splats* thanks to a long elastic band tied to his leg.

(It *must* be exciting: he's even gotten Jason to do it with him!)

However, Luke admits that even a bungee jump off Mount Everest is safer than the crazy thing he did in high school:

"Once," he says, "I jumped a motorcycle over two side-by-side Volkswagens just to see if I could do it . . . and I did."

Of course, he's quick to add that he'd been doing motorcycle jumps and tricks for years, and doesn't advise anyone doing something like that without loads of experience—and even *then*, only if they're slightly loco like him.

In fact, looking back and thinking how he could have destroyed himself, Luke is amazed that he did it at all, and certainly doesn't think he'd do it again. (If Aaron Spelling were there, he'd probably second that sentiment!)

That answered, you think of an even more unusual question to ask: what is Luke's favorite childhood memory?

Much to your surprise, that's an easy one. He says that the memory he cherishes the most is of one morning when he was four years old and he climbed up on his grandfather's lap to eat breakfast. He says that he's never felt as safe or content or just plain bathed in love as he did then.

You fight the urge to offer him *your* lap to sit on, realizing that that would be totally uncool. Instead, you take a deep breath and ask the Big One: is he *dating* anyone?

Luke smiles kind of forlornly and says, "Not right now." But not by choice, he says. *Beverly Hills, 90210* shoots such long hours and usually six days a week, so there really isn't time for him to have much of a social life.

But when he *does* go out, he says he likes to date "round, curvaceous" girls. He usually avoids bony ones because, he jokes, "I'm skinny enough for the two of us!"

Then he gets serious and adds, "Really, looks don't matter that much to me. The person inside is a lot more important than the one on the outside."

He says that glamour isn't something he looks for in a woman. He likes to be casual when he goes out—usually taking his date to a pizza parlor or a 1950s-style diner, both of which are serious weaknesses of his—and he says he gets along best with women who are easygoing in dress *and* manner.

As you'd expect, he points out that warmth, honesty, and a sense of humor are also very important traits of the women he goes out with.

Does he consider himself an old-fashioned kind of guy?

"Oh yes," he says emphatically. When he goes out, he walks right to the door to get his date (none of this honking-from-the-car stuff for Luke), escorts her back to the door when the night is through, and will give a girl a kiss on the first date—but that's it.

You cross your fingers and ask, Is he the marrying kind?

"I certainly am," he says, "and I like the idea of having a wife and a family. But I don't think it's fair to anyone at this point. It's a crazy business I'm in, and to do it wouldn't be right."

(Crazy is right! Because the show really started to climb in the ratings at the end of the first season, in the spring, Fox made the very unusual decision of shooting first-run episodes to show during the summer instead of reruns. That meant the stars had just a month off

90

before going back to work—barely enough time to rest and visit the folks back home before having to start learning the new scripts!)

So there's no woman in Luke's life (though he says he wouldn't mind meeting Linda Hamilton of *Terminator 2*), and you tell yourself, *At least there's hope!*

Chapter 23

You wait a moment for your heart to slow down and wonder if the air conditioning's gone off in here, or is Mrs. Perry's youngest son generating all that bodacious *heat*?

The hum of the air conditioner gives you your answer.

When your mind has cleared a bit, and you've drained your bottle of mineral water (which Luke promptly and courteously replaces with another), you ask:

What are his hobbies—other than going to parking lots and taking apart motor vehicles?

He says that cooking is something he loves to do, as well as fishing, mostly because it enables him to get out of the city and back into the country, where he's much more at home.

However, he doesn't hunt, and doesn't think it's a terribly cool thing to do unless you have to feed your family.

He says he also loves carpentry, designing furniture and building it from scratch.

When you point out that that's something movie superstar Harrison Ford *also* likes to do, Luke says that he'd be a supremely happy camper if his career went like Ford's has! (He's too *modest*, you tell yourself. It's Harrison Ford who should be so *lucky* to be taking off like Luke!)

What are the hobbies he'd *like* to take up?

He says he's started to study fencing, but has a long

way to go before he's really good with a sword.

Does he consider himself a funny guy?

"No," he says. "I'm fun-ish." In other words, he explains, no gags and practical jokes like Jason pulls, and *definitely* no wild parties. He doesn't like being around people who get drunk or stoned, and besides— he's got to get a good night's sleep so he can be alert on the set. He says he's just a lighthearted and free-spirited sorta guy when he's not working.

What is Luke's biggest *dislike*?

Luke says, "Crowds." Not that he's complaining, but he says, "Lately, because I have had to do a lot of things like interviews, public appearances, and things like that," he's had to deal with more and larger crowds . . . and he has to work hard not to get introverted in situations like that.

(Little did Luke know, a crowd beyond his wildest imaginings was just a few weeks away.)

You tell him that you noticed there were at least thirty-five other actors and crew members standing around when he was doing his scenes before. Isn't *that* a crowd? Didn't having all those people on the set *bother* him?

"No," he says. When he's acting in a part, he gets so deeply *into* the part that everyone but his fellow actors disappear. In fact, a couple of times while making this show, he says, "I found myself totally lost in my character and had to stop and think to myself, Wait a minute, this is make believe."

Remember earlier in the book, when we said that this actor *really* gets into a part? *That's* what we meant!

Speaking of acting, you wonder if, as a career, acting is everything he expected it to be.

In his wonderfully understated way, he laughs. "It beats other jobs I've had. Kissing girls for a living is not a bad way to go!"

And how about Hollywood? What does Luke think of it, and how do its values compare to the small town where he grew up?

His mood changes quickly, becomes much more subdued. He says he really doesn't like the part of Hollywood that is "decadently wealthy. People who really don't think anything about saying, 'I'm hungry. Let's fly to Paris for some food.' "

Luke plans to use a lot of whatever money he earns for charitable things. He says, "I truly believe that our generation has the responsibility and capability to make the necessary changes to make our world a better place," and he intends to do that. Luke has already given a great deal of money to the Multiple Sclerosis Society over the years, and he's presently doing other generous things, which we'll get into a little later.

Luke also believes that if he ever *does* get really super-rich, it won't change the way he lives or how he thinks.

How does he *know* that?

"Because of my background," he says. According to Luke, too many people go after the material things they need *first*, and then they "start looking for the emotional things they don't have, or the spiritual things they're missing." That, he says, is really difficult.

In his case, Luke says he did it the other way around. He built his character up before he started building his bank account, and his advice to young people is "to attain all the nonmaterial things first."

Like what?

Like respect for others, he says. Respect for nature, and self-respect. These, he insists (and rightly so!) are more important than monetary riches.

Luke has been extremely open (just as you always *knew* he'd be), and feeling that you can get a little more personal, you ask how close he is to his brother and sister.

"Very," he says, "though it's difficult for us to see each other because I live here, my sister lives in Ohio, and Tom lives in Chicago. But we try."

Was Tom involved in Operation Desert Storm, you wonder.

"No," says Luke, obviously relieved. "But when we were having trouble with Libya, he was over there." Luke adds that he doesn't worry about Tom, though—not because he doesn't care but "because he wouldn't want me to."

Obviously, Tom Perry is every inch as giving and wonderful as his brother!

What about his sister Amy? What does she do?

"She's married and very happy," he says, then politely but firmly explains that he really would prefer not to say any more about them, or about his stepsister Emily. He tells you that each of his three siblings cherishes their privacy, and he doesn't want to do anything to jeopardize that.

You can't help but respect his wishes . . . and respect Luke for protecting his brother and sisters!

Okay. You've found out some of the things you've been wondering about Luke. But there are things you want to know about Dylan as well, and since the clock is running, you turn your attention from Luke to his thoughts on the character he plays.

Chapter 24

Still sitting in Luke Perry's comfy dressing room, you ask the question that *everyone* wonders: how alike are Luke Perry and Dylan McKay?

From the time you've spent with Luke, talking or just watching him on the set, you can see that there *are* many differences: Luke smiles a lot more, and he's a lot more giving to those around him. He also doesn't say "man" as much.

But you know there must be other differences as well as a number of similarities, and you're dying to know what he says.

The actor has been pretty relaxed until now, throwing off answers with ease. Now, however, that gorgeously high forehead wrinkles in thought. Luke sits back, one leg stretched in front of him, the other on the couch, his knee upraised. He's holding his second bottle of mineral water loosely by its neck, his wrist draped across his knee.

After thinking for a long moment, he says, "It's a difficult question to answer because there are so many parts to it."

He says that the main thing he and Dylan have in common is "I don't take too much of anything seriously and neither does Dylan." Also, he says, "Dylan is a little distant from life and society and I guess I am too, in a lot of ways."

Luke points out, however, that the *reason* they both tend to keep to themselves is different. He says that Dylan stays apart from society because he's bitter about how he's been treated by his mother and by so many other people. Dylan wants what society can't give him—love and attention—so he gives it the cold shoulder.

In Luke's case, he stands back from Hollywood society because he has something precious that he doesn't want to lose: ironically, like Brandon Walsh, he doesn't want the superficial, materialistic standards of Hollywood to corrupt the Midwestern values he grew up with.

"Hollywood," he says, "doesn't really offer that much for me other than the business and the life surrounding that."

Apart from those two qualities, Luke says that the only other way he and Dylan are alike is in their curiosity about people and what makes them tick—including themselves.

"Sometimes," says the actor, "I don't know exactly what I'm looking for, and neither does he. But that doesn't stop either of us from looking."

However, in thinking about it, Luke says that there are probably many, many more differences than similarities between himself and the disenfranchised former substance-abuser.

Top of the list, says Luke, is that he himself isn't really a drinker (nor does he use drugs). Elaborating on what he said before about wild parties and substance abuse, he says, "I've seen their terrible effects on others more than once in my life," and he urges people to stay away from them regardless of the kinds of pressures they're under.

Also, as we've seen, unlike Dylan, Luke is very much loved by his mother and family.

Other than that, Luke says, "Dylan always acts like he knows what he's doing, but the truth is he doesn't. He really doesn't. I guess I'm that way in *some* respects, but the difference is I don't *pretend* that I know everything. Because I don't. I mean, who does?"

You ask Luke if he can give you an example of Dylan being all-thumbs without realizing it.

Luke thinks—wrinkling that Mount Rushmore forehead again—takes a swig of water, and says, "Look at his relationships with women. Not in getting women, but once you have someone, what do you do with them?" Luke says Dylan *really* doesn't have a clue, because until Brenda, there's never been anyone in his life who has needed him . . . who has *shown* him what to do. And the two of them haven't really done gold-medal-winning jobs of helping each other either.

You resist the temptation to raise your hand and volunteer to go on the show and teach Dylan how people can care about other people.

Luke continues talking about the differences between himself and Dylan.

"I didn't grow up rich like he did. And I'm not angry. Dylan's pretty angry, rebellious—I'm not like that. I'm a pretty happy guy, I think.

"But I *like* Dylan," he stresses. He says that Dylan's "not one-dimensional. He's different . . . very literate, wise beyond his years. He doesn't really like a lot of the people around him, except for Brandon and Brenda, which is why he doesn't open up much. I'm like him in *that* way because I watch and listen a lot, as opposed to just running off at the mouth. You learn a lot more that way."

You know about the experiences that Luke brought to the part of Dylan, but you wonder if there's anything that Dylan has given Luke, apart from the obvious— the devotion of millions of fans.

"Sure," he says. "Playing Dylan has given me the chance to experience a lot of my fantasies."

No joke!

He gets to be cool in most situations, gets to hang with a very pretty lady, and enjoys a close friendship with Brandon. Who *wouldn't* mind trying a character like that on for size?

Chapter 25

Luke has gotten very quiet when discussing Dylan—quieter, even, than when he was talking about his family! And then you realize just how close actors sometimes feel to the characters they play, even if they *don't* have a lot in common.

What about Dylan's high school experiences? you ask. Has Luke been able to draw on anything from his own high school when playing Dylan?

Luke bursts out laughing. "No," he says. "My high school experience was so *hugely* different. We had classes on birthing cows and driving tractors!"

The topic of Luke's relationship with Dylan having pretty much been exhausted, you ask how Luke gets along with the other actors.

The star deadpans, "I beat Jason up on a regular basis."

When he notices the look of horror that crosses your face, he laughs and says, "No—just kidding. We're cool.

"How does everyone get along?" he repeats the question. "Well, it's a great set to be on, even though sometimes it gets real tense. I guess it's just the pressure of having to make a show that quickly."

(Most of the episodes are shot in just six days. Compare that to the *months* it takes to shoot a motion picture!)

"But everyone's basically happy," Luke goes on, "and we do get along. There are no major fights going down."

Unfortunately, one thing that *is* going down is the time you have to chat with Luke: it's almost up. You manage to squeeze in one more question.

"Luke," you ask, "do you think that teenagers today are as irresponsible as so many people say they are?"

He fastens those chocolate-brown eyes on you and shakes his head slowly.

"A lot of people forget that high school kids are intelligent," he says. "All they remember (*from when they were in high school*) is the zits, problems, and no self-confidence. But come on! I don't think there is any social group that is as aware as teenagers!"

And don't think that Luke is just full o' beans: he knows what he's talking about. In addition to charity appearances (more on that very soon), Luke goes to high schools and talks to the kids about matters of importance to them and to the world.

Luke describes how, just recently, he and several other young celebrities went to the *real* Beverly Hills High School. The occasion was Buckle Up America week, and they visited the school in order to give an auditorium full of students some pointers about intelligent driving habits.

Given his long experience with motor vehicles, it's a subject with which Luke is very well acquainted, as you know—and which he feels very, very strongly about!

Wearing a "Traffic Safety Now" tee, Luke listened intently while Jeremy Licht (*The Hogan Family*), David Faustino (*Married . . . with Children*), Jenny Beck (*Guns of Paradise*), Kellie Martin (*Life Goes On*), and Soleil Moon Frye (*Punky Brewster*) all gave short, to-the-point speeches about good driving habits and some of their own personal experiences.

Then Luke rose slowly, walked over to the podium, leaned toward the mike, and addressed the packed, silent auditorium.

He said, "On our show, we have a wonderful lady who does props. Anything you ever see in my hands, she gives to me. Her name is Barbie [Kirk], and she's a great lady."

His voice cracking with emotion, Luke went on.

"Recently, she was involved in a multi-car crash on the freeway, and three of the cars were totaled; two of the people in the other automobiles were injured severely.

"The worst injury that Barbie has is one she's very proud of. She has a big bruise that goes right across here [he crisscrosses his chest] where she was strapped into her seat belt.

"She walked away virtually unscathed because she had her seat belt on. Proof positive that it works. If everybody gets together, and we work on this seat belt thing, and it's not hard . . . it's on, you're safe, you can drive.

"Remember that. It only takes two seconds. *I* think your life is worth it, and I hope you think so too.

"If you want to live," he summed up his short but very effective speech, "strap yourself in! It's *that* simple."

He sat down to thunderous applause, and the satisfying feeling that he might have done some good here—that maybe, just maybe, his talk might save a few lives.

Truly, Luke and Jason *co*-rule.

There's a moment of silence in the room and, feeling tingly all over, you thank him for his time, courtesy, and thoughtful answers.

You rise and he rises, too, thanks you for being interested in what he has to say, and walks you to the door. He says he'll see you later, back on the set.

The brilliant sun momentarily blinds you as you step from the dressing room—though you can't help but think that the star up in the sky isn't nearly as hot as the one you're leaving behind.

But you don't have time (or reason) to grieve *too* much: Jason Priestley's dressing room is just a few steps away, and you quickly walk toward it.

Chapter 26

You rap quietly on the door.

"Yo, come in," Jason says cheerfully.

You enter the small room and look to where Jason is standing, still wearing the porkpie hat he'd been fooling with on the soundstage.

He's on the phone, and you wait a few seconds while he finishes his conversation. When he hangs up, he stands, doffs his hat, and extends an arm to the little couch on which he was sitting.

He offers you a drink, and you accept a Diet Coke, which is what he's having. After you sit down, he asks what Luke asked: if you're having fun.

Seeing as how Jason's a kidder, you take a chance with him and say, "Yes. It's almost as much fun as being on the set of the *The CBS Evening News*."

Jason flops down on the couch beside you, tossing aside the hat, and, without missing a beat, says in a deep, sonorous, Walter Cronkite-y voice, "In Hollywood today, young actor Jason Priestley was arrested after killing a visitor for suggesting that a network news desk was more interesting than a visit to West Hollywood High . . . "

You laugh, realizing that you should've known better than to try and one-up master jokester Jason Bradford Priestley!

But he appreciated *your* joke and says so, and, perfectly relaxed, you begin chitchatting—starting with where he was born and getting that squid-fisherman-for-a-father answer.

Jason, who was a flip, friendly dude on the set, is positively outgoing and super-warm now that the pressure of shooting the show is momentarily off.

He kicks back, sips his soda, cracks jokes (no kidding!), and makes you feel completely at ease.

In fact, it's tough to get on to the serious stuff, but you know you have to: once again, your time *is* limited.

As with Luke, you start with the *fun* kind of questions, like . . .

Where does Jason live?

He has a home in Woodland Hills (a pleasant, mall-dotted suburb of Los Angeles).

In addition to the Yamaha and now a Harley, what's Jason driving these days?

"An Alfa Romeo," says he—which is a *very* hot sports car. "I love cars," he adds. "They're my passion!"

His favorite color?

"Black," he says.

That gives you chills, 'cuz you stop and think how dynamite Jason would look entirely in black leather.

What's his favorite TV show? Is it *Jeopardy!*, just like his friend Luke?

Nothing quite as intellectual, says Jason. It's *Married . . . with Children*—and *not*, he assures us, because it happens to be on the Fox Network. He just thinks it's the funniest show on television.

We know what Luke's favorite movies are, so you ask Jason, What are his?

He says he has two: *A Clockwork Orange* (remember, the book was also a fave) and director David Lynch's bizarre murder mystery *Blue Velvet* starring (who else?) Jason's hero Dennis Hopper.

We know he adores hamburgers and fries, but we hear he's also a wizard in the kitchen. When he's

105

not playing lord of the fries, what does Jason like to cook?

"Mexican and Chinese dishes are my specialties," he boasts. "I can make Mexican food like a maniac!" Since moving to L.A., he confesses that these have been catching up to burgers at the top of his hit list.

Apart from hockey and rugby, what is Jason's favorite sport? (Hope you're sitting down while you're reading this, 'cuz the answer's gonna surprise you!)

Jason says that he loves playing golf, and he wishes he had more time to get out there and improve his game.

Apart from golf (*golf?!,* you're still thinkin'), what does he wish he had more time to do?

Perfect his drum-playing. He says he's only gotten serious with the instrument fairly recently (inspired, in part, by Brian Green's father, who's a professional drummer), and he wishes he could beat his set more often.

He'd also like to be able to spend more time in Las Vegas, a city he really digs.

Okay—you've touched on some interesting likes and dislikes, but it's time to probe a little deeper . . .

Chapter 27

You know it's a kind of rude question, but you really have to know: does Jason ever suffer from an ego problem—like thinking he's better than everyone because of his looks and talent?

Never, he insists—and he's so sincere that you believe him and trust him.

"I don't get up in the morning and look in the mirror and say, 'Hey, Jay baby, lookin' good today,'" he tells you, repeating something he's said before.

"In fact," says Jason, because of the long hours he keeps, he claims that what he *really* does is, "I get up and say, 'Where's the Visine?'"

What about the money and fame he's getting now? Hasn't *that* affected him in the teensiest bit?

"No way," he says, shaking his head. "They're just trappings. I'm really a simple guy with simple tastes and a very simple lifestyle. I don't need to have all the status symbols that go with that.

"Look," he says, "I'm an actor. *That's* what makes me happy and I'm lucky because I can get up every morning and go to a job that I love. It's something that I have a passion for and that I enjoy doing."

He says that while he truly adores his fans and is very appreciative of them, the wealth and popularity he's currently enjoying really "are secondary. My lifestyle and my attitudes haven't changed in the slightest from what they were before."

What about being recognized? That *has* to make it a little more difficult for Jason to go out in public.

"A little," he admits. "But I can still go to a movie or go to the shopping mall, which is good because my private life is very important to me and I like to have some privacy. Sometimes, when you get really famous, you lose that." (How does he get through unseen? He doesn't shave and definitely does *not* dress like Brandon!)

If someone does recognize him, how does he handle it?

As courteously as possible, he says. "I can be at the gas station and someone comes up and asks for an autograph or to take a picture with me." He says he does it, but he always reminds himself that it shouldn't give him a swelled head. "That doesn't make me an incredible person and it doesn't make my ego grow. It's all very flattering, but really—it's just what happens because of my job."

He says that he's learned one important thing above all since coming to Southern California. The key to being happy in Hollywood, he's discovered, is: "You have to work to be a success as an actor, not as a celebrity." And that's what he does, every day of his life.

Three cheers for JP! Definitely *not* the attitude of a major egomeister! In fact, he's so modest you want to grab him and say, "Jason, you dummy: you *are* an incredible person!"

Speaking of ego, you risk his wrath by asking if it ever bothers him that he's not as tall as a lot of other heartthrobs.

Negative, says he. As a matter of fact, he points out that he encouraged the producers when they suggested doing a show about Brandon not being tall enough to make the basketball team.

Jason believes that what makes a person big is the size of his or her heart, not the size of their body.

How much fan mail does he receive each week?

"About five hundred letters," he says—though it's been growing a little every week.

(For the record, Luke recently has been receiving *one thousand* letters a week. But is Jason jealous? Not on your life! He says it's like when Mr. Spock used to get the largest chunk of the *Star Trek* fan mail: Jason says quiet, mysterious guys *always* attract the most attention!

Anyway, he says he's really happy for Luke. How *could* he be jealous of the success of such a nice guy and good friend?)

From Bev Hills to the U.S.S. *Enterprise*—this has become a far-ranging chat indeed! But though you've spanned the cosmos, there's still more you want to know . . .

Chapter 28

Tick-tick-tick—

You wish you could stop time and stay here talkin' with Jason forever, but you know that'd be impractical, not to mention selfish: he deserves some time alone and beside, if he doesn't get back to work, there won't be any more episodes of *Beverly Hills, 90210*!

So you dive into a couple of meaty questions, starting with—

What does he like most about acting?

He answers without hesitation, "The excitement of it! In a regular job, many people reach a point where they know their work inside and out, and then they can no longer improve. But in acting, there is unlimited potential for growth!"

He's quick to add that, like Luke, he believes that self-improvement in *all* areas of life is tremendously important.

"I've never been fully satisfied with any performance I've ever given," he says. Jason admits that it can be frustrating, setting increasingly higher goals for himself, but he says, "It also forces me to improve, which I think is the most important thing in life."

One way he does this in his work is by making a point of watching the "dailies": the footage that was shot the day before. A lot of actors don't bother with this, but Jason feels it's the best way to see what it is you're doing right and wrong.

110

Does he have any long-term ambitions other than acting?

"Yes, I do!" he says enthusiastically. "I'd like to direct movies and TV shows in the future.

"It's just another form of expression," explains this talented artist. "What I do is very visual, but as a director you go to another level of physical expression. You use the camera as a tool of expression."

Another ambition, he says, is that he, Luke and Ian want to open up a restaurant one day.

In Beverly Hills? you ask.

Not likely, says Jay. Whenever the show ends its run (which won't be for years and years), he says he'll probably want to get *away* from zipper 90210 for a while.

Speaking of the show, he's got to be pleased by the success of *Beverly Hills, 90210*. But is he happy with the quality of the series?

"I'm very proud of the show," he says. "I think we deal with a lot of the problems teenagers face, in a very realistic way. We talk about things that other shows don't dare to—the tough stuff."

Such as? you ask.

He grows very serious. "Well," he begins, "I know when I grew up it was a whole different set of problems from today. Kids today face potentially life-threatening things. You think about AIDS, you think about crack— all these things that I never had to worry about.

"On our show we've been able to address some of those issues (*and we'll do even more of that next season*) and not be preachy about it. We don't say, 'Don't do this or that.' We simply show these things and what the possible effects can be."

What does Jason think about Brandon?

"He's a normal guy who's been thrust into the seemingly glamorous, fast-paced Beverly Hills lifestyle, but he's secure enough with who he is that he won't let go of his Midwestern values and morals."

Brandon seems so *mature*, you point out.

"Yes," Jason agrees. "He's very intelligent, and I think that's where his maturity comes from."

Is he the kind of guy you, personally, would want to hang with?

Jason says that he would. "I like Brandon. I've kind of got a soft spot for him."

And *is* the Brander as perfect a guy as he seems to be, or is there some really nasty stuff hidden deep down inside?

Jason grins. "In the beginning, he was a little *too* righteous. But Brandon's becoming a lot more fallible, a lot more human."

The actor thinks for a moment, then adds, "Yeah, Brandon's got a bad side. We just haven't seen it yet. We saw a *little* of it when he got drunk and crashed his car," Jason says, but then promises, "there's more."

You remark that you can't wait to see what lies behind the Brandonburg Gate, and he groans at your joke. So you move on.

Will Andrea and Brandon ever become an item?

"Could be." He winks. "You'll have to wait and see!" (The smart money is betting on *yes*.)

How much control does he have over what happens to Brandon in the scripts?

"Some," he says. "I don't think there's anyone who knows Brandon better than I do." Jason says that when he sees something in the script that doesn't seem very Brandonesque to him, "I'll say, 'Brandon wouldn't do it that way. He'd probably do it *this* way.' The writers and the producers are very receptive to the input of the actors," he says, "which is nice."

Does he ever suggest story ideas?

"Some of us suggest things," he says, "but we have a great staff of writers that takes care of most of it."

How does he feel about his fellow cast members?

"We're all friends," he says enthusiastically, though he says he hangs "mostly with Luke and Ian. We're all about the same age, and we have a lot of the same interests."

Like?

Sports, he says. Cars, too. And, of course, the ladies.

Chapter 29

With only a few minutes left, and the conversation really clicking, you decide to ask some heavier questions.

Is he interested in marriage?

"Absolutely," Jason says, though right now he describes himself as "playing the field . . . responsibly." For a while, he was dating actress Robin Lively, who had appeared on *Twin Peaks*—but that broke up because his schedule doesn't leave him any more time than Luke has for dating. And guess where Jason met Robin? On the set of *Teen Angel Returns. She* played the girl he came to earth to help.

Jason jokes, "Actually, there's this part of my contract that says I can't have a social life!"

As a result of having to work day in and day out, he says he doesn't see marriage happening anytime real soon.

When it does, is there any kind of girl that he *wouldn't* be interested in?

Just one, he says: *raiding* the field is a big taboo to Jason.

"I think if you go after another guy's girl, it's bad karma and somebody will do that to your girlfriend in return someday."

What about girls who drink? Does that turn him off?

He says that *anyone* who relies heavily on alcohol turns him off. "People think you drink alcohol to have a good time. But if you're confused and insecure and things are happening to you that you don't understand, drinking and those basic teenage insecurities can be a lethal combination."

In the strongest possible terms, he urges all teens to think hard about *not* drinking. And you can only say a heartfelt *amen* to that.

What about charities?

He says that for the last year or so, he's been devoting as much time as possible to raising money for Pediatric AIDS (children who have the terrible disease) and visiting sick kids in the hospital.

Jason says, "If I can just bring a smile to the face of a kid that hasn't smiled in a long time, that's very important."

Jason also says that just recently, he and Luke and costar Brian Green were on the same team in a celebrity softball game that raised nearly a half-million dollars for the T. J. Martell Foundation—money that would go to AIDS and cancer research. Though their team lost by one run, Jason says that it was very rewarding getting out there and raising money for such a worthwhile cause.

Jason says that he and Luke plan to do it again, as often as their busy schedules allow.

And speaking of busy schedules—

Jason has been too polite to say anything, but you've been sitting here for over twenty minutes. Twenty minutes here, twenty minutes with Luke: lunch hour is nearly over, and these two guys have given up a big, two-liter-sized gulp of it to you!

You feel a little selfish having intruded on their private time (time when they could've been studying their lines or resting or making phone calls or even having a bite to eat), and you rise quickly and apologize to Jason.

He tells you not to be silly, it was his pleasure having you here.

The hunky Hills hero rises, and before he can walk you to the door, the phone rings. It's just as well: you didn't want him to see your legs wobbling from weakness as you walked away.

He says he'll see you back on the set and waves as he scoops up the receiver. Reluctantly, you show yourself out.

Once again the sunlight startles you, and the heat outside doesn't make it any easier for you to catch your breath.

You stand there for a few seconds, chilled to the max, thinking how truly incredible these two guys are. They *could* have been annoyed to have to talk to you, or put out or just plain rude. So many of the stars you talk to are like that.

But not these two. They were easy-to-talk-to gentlemen, and you find yourself respecting them more than ever.

Just then, Shannen steps out of her black BMW, which is parked in her own private slot. She obviously used her lunch hour to do some shopping, and as she walks by, headed back to the set, she waves.

"You going to be sticking around?" she asks cheerfully.

I could live here, you think, but you say you are, and she says that if there's anything you want to ask her about the show or her costars, not to be shy. Just step right over when she's free.

You thank her, fully intending to take her up on the offer. She disappears into the soundstage, and you're alone again with your thoughts.

Then, when you've just about collected your wits—which have been wilted and numbed by forty minutes of Luke 'n' Jason heaven—you realize with horror that after all that time in the dressing room with Jason, and all the questions you asked, *you forgot the most important one of all*:

You forgot to ask Jason what part of his body he'd change if he could!

You look back at the dressing room. You can't intrude on his privacy by going back and asking—so, quickly, you rush ahead to catch up with Shannen.

Chapter 30

The bright lights have been turned off in the sound-stage. But as your eyes adjust, you can see that crew members and actors alike are beginning to return from lunch.

Shannen is standing off to one side. She's talking with Jennie Garth, who wasn't needed this morning and has only just arrived.

You don't want to interrupt, so you sidle over behind them and just kind of eavesdrop.

The two women are talking about the eighteenth birthday party Tori Spelling recently threw for herself at the hip, hot Los Angeles club Bar One. From what you gather, it was a radical affair!

The theme was "Casino Night," and all of the *Beverly Hills, 90210* stars (not to mention 150 other guests) took turns having fun with the big roulette wheels that were everywhere.

There was a deejay on hand, playing all the popular songs (even some Jerry Lee Lewis for Luke), and a humongous buffet with everything from prime rib to pasta to turkey to lobster tails to shrimp.

Jason—who, as you've noticed, takes his work very seriously—spent a lot of time talking about the show with producer Aaron Spelling. (You really do wish the Priest-man would *relax* more!)

Brian Green, a major rap music fanatic, spent most of the time getting down, jiving the night away on the dance floor. (You realize, now, that he wasn't acting when he seemed to be having such a blast on the show's prom episode. He really *was* having fun! Though you've got to admit, it was tough watching cute Bri on that episode while Luke was nearby, cutting a rug and looking splendiferous in his tux . . .)

David Silver spent his time dancing, eating, and studying the surroundings, getting ideas for his *own* birthday, which was coming up.

Luke stayed near his date for most of the night—which was none other than Tori! She wasn't even angry with him when he arrived two hours late because an interview ran over.

Shannen says that when Luke *did* arrive, he hurried through the door, dressed in a sports jacket and white tee, rushed over to Tori, kissed her on the cheek, and said, "I love history."

When Tori asked *why*, he said, "Well—like now *I'm* history 'cause I'm late."

Tori laughed and forgave him: she said that at least he was in time to offer the toast before she cut the cake!

That the Lukester did, and gladly. First he whispered a private little wish into his hon's ear, then he gave an out-loud one—the kind you'd expect one actor to give to another.

He said, "I wish Tori health, happiness . . . and lots of work!"

Then Tori blew out the candles, cut the cake, scooped up some icing . . . and slapped late Luke in the mouth with a handful of the vanilla frosting!

Luke was surprised, but as Jason doubled over with laughter, Luke laughed, sucked the icing down, wiped a big smudge off his chin, and turned to Jason, who was standing right beside him.

"I expected something like that from *you!*" he said to prankster Jase.

119

Mr. Priestley stopped laughing long enough to say, "Wait, man—the night's not over yet!"

According to Shannen, the two dudes watched each other all night, waiting for the other one to do something.

(Later, when you see Tori on the *Beverly Hills, 90210* set, you ask her if there's anything "going on" between her and Luke.

She smiles coyly and says, "Luke and I are really close, good friends on and off the set."

Uh . . . does that mean you're seeing each other? you ask.

Tori's smile turns Twentieth Century-Foxy, but that's all she'll say about the relationship.)

From everything that Shannen and Jennie have said about the party, you can tell it was a groovy affair, one that you would've given your collection of Jason and Luke pinups to attend! (All except for a few *choice* pics, that is.)

When Shannen happens to notice you standing off to the side, she gestures quickly for you to come over. You don't need a second invite, and hurry over to where the actresses are standing, just outside the bedroom set.

Shannen introduces you to Jennie, the former teen beauty pageant competitor who is every bit as beautiful in person as she seems on TV.

Jennie gives you an enthusiastic "Hi!" and offers you her hand; the warm welcome shows just how different Jennie is from snobby Kelly. You're impressed—as you've been with everyone, so far—at how accessible she seems. No *I'm a star* trip. Jennie Garth is just plain folks.

Jennie tells Shannen that if they get out early today ("Fat chance," Shannen groans), she'd like to go buy some clothes—"power shopping," she calls it. She asks if Shannen would like to come along.

120

Shannen says that she'd tentatively planned to hit the stores with Tori, and that maybe all three of them can go together.

Jennie says that'll be great and excuses herself to get ready for the afternoon's work. When she's gone, you spend a few moments talking to Shannen.

Chapter 31

Being an eager reporter, if not a very *smooth* one, you ask Shannen Doherty right off the bat if *she* knows what Jason would change about his heavenly bod if he could?

She winces as if she's in pain. She has no idea and says, goodness gracious, what could he *want* to change?

Your sentiments exactly, you tell her, but you've heard there *is* something.

She can't help you, so instead you talk a bit about the show. For example, you're just *dying* to know what it's like to kiss Luke Perry!

Shannen laughs. "Girls come up to me all the time and ask that," she says. "They say, 'You're so lucky! You get to kiss Luke!' "

Shannen says that, yes, she *is* lucky . . . and yes, she loves kissing Luke. But she's quick to point out, "There's also about forty people watching you as you do that!"

In other words, it's a kiss . . . but it's *not* exactly an intimate moment, no matter what it looks like on TV.

You ask how close she and Luke are off-camera.

She's says they're close, but that he's "more like a brother." She admits that the ones who are really closest to Luke are Jason and Ian. Shannen says that her best friend among the cast members is Tori.

Just then, seemingly from out of nowhere, Tori wanders over.

"Yes, we're best friends," says the statuesque actress as she sashays toward you, but then she offers to tell you some dirt about her best friend.

Shannen seems surprised. *Dirt? What dirt?*

Tori puts on her smuggest, most Donna-like expression and says, "Shannen . . . "

You wait, holding your breath for the hot scoop—

"Shannen," she repeats, "—*loves* junk food!"

You seem disappointed by the revelation, and Tori bursts into laughter.

It's true, Shannen says, and Tori admits that she *hates* her friend for that, because "she eats constantly and never gains an ounce!"

Shannen and Tori both laugh, and when you ask Tori if the show is always as much fun to make as it seems, she says, "It's a *lot* of fun! Most of the time, it's not like going to work at all—I look forward to getting on the set so I can visit with my friends, just like this."

After the two women talk a bit about the upcoming scenes, Tori saunters toward the set to talk to the director, who's just returned from lunch.

You have just enough time to ask two more questions: What does she think of Jason?

She says, "He's gorgeous. He has those *eyes*—!"

So, would she *date* him?

It isn't really an issue, she says, because she's involved pretty seriously with a real estate developer.

Now the other cast members begin arriving as well, and Shannen waves a little good-bye as she leaves to prepare for work.

As she heads toward the script supervisor to check on some of her lines, you're amazed—just as you were with Jennie—at how different Shannen is from Brenda, how outgoing and *confident* she seems!

123

You turn toward the big soundstage door. Gabrielle Carteris has arrived, already made up and rarin' to go, and after checking in with the director and saying hi to the other cast members, she sits down off to the side of the set.

You tiptoe over and introduce yourself, and she invites you to pull up a chair. You happen to grab the one that says "Luke Perry" on the back, and you shiver as you plant your unworthy self in it.

So, you ask her, jumping right to the important stuff (you never know when she's going to be called away): what's it like to do a love scene with Jason Priestley?

Her eyes light up and she says, "He's a great guy and he kisses fine too!"

Just "*fine*" you ask?

Gabrielle leans closer—like she's about to confide a big secret—and answers that she doesn't want to say anything more because "I have a boyfriend whom I care about very much. I only kiss Jason when we're doing a scene together."

Aha! She said that Jason kisses "*fine*" because she doesn't want to make a certain boyfriend jealous. And that makes perfect sense. What guy *wouldn't* be a little concerned if his lady spent the day smoochin' and snugglin' with the very proper Priestley?

When asked, Gabrielle says that she's also very fond of Luke, and felt close to him from day one due to the fact that they'd both done soaps in New York.

"When we first met," she says, "we started talking about some of our friends on the East Coast and found out that we had some mutual friends. That brought us together really quickly."

In fact, she says that if there's anything she regrets about the recent success of the show, it's that she and Luke and the other cast members can't go out to dinner anymore, something they all enjoyed doing when the show first started and was at the bottom of the ratings.

"We're finding that going out is getting harder and harder because we get recognized a lot more quickly."

As you're sitting there, you see that the other guys have started to show up—Ian, Brian, and Douglas. Gabrielle notices that you've been a *little* distracted by the Bev Hills stallions, so she graciously offers to walk over there and introduce you.

Even though you feel unworthy, you're on your feet and ready before she's finished offering!

Chapter 32

As Gabrielle approaches the guys with you in tow, they all stop to say hello to her in unison:

"Good afternoon, Gabrielle!"

You smile and your eyes don't know where to go first. They end up just bopping all over—from strong, six-foot one-inch, blue-eyed Ian to cute, five-foot-seven Brian, to angelic-looking five-foot five-inch Douglas.

Remember that extravagant buffet at Tori's party? Well . . . *forget* it! *This* is the kind of buffet you want to see at *your* next party.

Fortunately for your ping-ponging eyes, the question of where to settle is answered as Luke strides into the makeshift soundstage—Mr. Serious, still studying his script.

Your eyes lock on him like cruise missiles.

Without stopping, Luke high-fives the others, smiles at you, and continues to the set. Your eyes don't leave him the entire time.

Then Jason returns, and once again your baby blues know just where to go. He slaps Ian on the back, stops to talk for a second, then makes his way to the set. He flashes a smile at you as he passes, and for a moment you're paralyzed with ecstasy—

So much so, in fact, that by the time you remember your question about the body part, Jason's already busy with the other cast members and the director on the set.

Curses—foiled again!

Feeling like a dork, you follow the other actors over and sit back in Luke's chair—this time because he's offered it to you personally.

You watch, entranced, as filming resumes on the vacation episode. And as you do, you marvel not only at how professional everyone is, but how proud they all must be.

Though *Beverly Hills, 90210* is a runaway smash hit now, it wasn't always that way.

When Fox put the show on last October, in a Thursday night slot, it was hardly seen by *anyone*. Creamed by *Cheers*, it was at the very bottom of the ratings, and for a while it seemed as though the patient—this aware, important series—would die.

Why did such a terrific show have such a difficult time catching on?

To begin with, it came on the air with one strike against it: critics were actually slamming the show before they'd seen a *single* episode! The reason? Aaron Spelling.

As Ian has said a number of times, "It was aggravating, hearing our show being criticized because it was being produced by the same man who made shows like *Fantasy Island* and *The Love Boat*.

"What critics never took into consideration was that Mr. Spelling had also produced *Family*, one of the most important contemporary dramas in the history of television."

Ian's right, but that didn't stop the critics from prejudging *Beverly Hills, 90210*.

Strike two against the show was its time slot, which gave Jason an uncomfortable feeling of *déjà vu*: he knew from bitter experience how tough it was going up against a hit show!

Unlike *Sister Kate*, however, *Beverly Hills, 90210* had a low viewership partly because the Fox network

127

didn't make people aware of the show. The producers *knew* they had a potential blockbuster if only viewers knew it was on!

On several occasions, Charles Rosin has talked to the press about the unhappy period after the show first premiered.

"We were so marginal for so long," he says, meaning the show hung precariously between being renewed and being canceled. Finally, he says, early in 1991 he and the rest of the creative team "went into the network and said, 'Listen, unless you start promoting us, no one's going to know we're here.'"

Fox executives knew he was right, and after huddling together and trying to figure out what to do, they decided to do three things.

First, they'd leave the show on Thursday nights, to take advantage of the audience that was tuning in to *The Simpsons*, where they'd promote it heavily. Hopefully, those viewers would stick around to watch *Beverly Hills, 90210*.

Second, they decided, as Ian puts it, to let the writers tackle even *more* difficult subjects on the show.

"And not just 'sensational' subjects that would look good in the *TV Guide* blurbs," he says, "but things that really affect and concern high school kids, like shoplifting, racism, marital strife, and sexual responsibility."

The young actor gives enormous credit to Fox for this, stating that the network "was more interested in the quality of the show than in producing a lot of big ratings right off the bat. At one of the other networks, we would probably have been canceled halfway through the first season!"

Sad, but true!

Third, and perhaps most important of all, Fox also opted to trot out their secret weapons, especially stars Priestley and Perry, and make teenaged America *aware* of the pair and their supreme coolness!

The two stars worked their tails off doing publicity. They went on national and local talk shows. They gave interviews to newspapers. Reporters from teen magazines and TV magazines were invited to the set and allowed to meet the stars.

By February, the incredible occurred: the show didn't just begin to climb in the ratings, it took off like a shaken-up bottle of Jason's ever-present Diet Coke!

Before the month was out, the series was doing better than the shows on major networks ABC and CBS, and was only barely trailing *Cheers* in its time period— *Cheers,* the number-one-rated television show in the nation! Its other competition, *Gabriel's Fire, Father Dowling,* and *The Trials of Rosie O'Neill,* was getting seriously whumped whenever they were on.

That was when Fox made the gutsy move of ordering new episodes of *Beverly Hills, 90210* to air throughout the summer and straight into fall, without a break. When other shows were in reruns, viewers would have a chance to sample fresh goods on Fox! That made a total order of *thirty* new episodes of the series—a move almost unprecedented in TV history!

By April, research showed that Jason was the hottest young star in the country, with Luke nipping at his heels; by May, depending on which survey you checked, the two were tied as the new heroes of young America!

Jason, Shannen, Ian, Gabrielle, and Jennie were sent to England on a whirlwind publicity tour to increase awareness of *Beverly Hills, 90210* and also to stir up interesting photo opportunities to get press coverage. The tour proved to be a tremendous success in every way.

Wherever the young stars went, hordes of fans turned out to greet them. As a result the ratings began to soar.

Yet, even though they were aware of the rocketing ratings and the ever-increasing flood of fan mail, the stars weren't quite aware of how *fanatic* their fans were.

Take, for example, Luke's ill-fated trips to a couple of shopping malls just this past spring and summer . . .

Chapter 33

Luke and Gabrielle were flown in to Bellevue, Washington, in May, to make an appearance at Bellevue Square. There, they were supposed to talk to some fans and sign a few autographs.

Sure, sure—Luke said he doesn't like crowds. But there are some things you have to do for other people. And in this case, his fellow cast members and the producers were depending on Luke to go out and help promote the show.

Luke, being Luke, would never do anything to let his coworkers down. So he and Gabrielle went, and— *wham*!

Instead of the thousand or so Lukies *tops* the organizers had been expecting, the actors showed up and were rushed by more than *four* thousand screaming, clutching, fainting fans!

Luke didn't get to do much at the mall before he was grabbed by security people who were concerned for his safety. They literally threw him into a laundry hamper and carried Luke out to his limousine, in secret.

Gabrielle says, "I know it sounds funny now, but at the time everyone was pretty scared."

Okay, thought Luke and the producers—things got a *little* out of hand. No one was expecting that many people, and it was only one mall, and the next time things would be different.

At the next mall, there would be more security and everyone would be better prepared.

Right.

Actually, everyone *was* prepared at the Fashion Mall in small, charming Plantation, Florida. Instead of the thirteen security guards they'd been planning to have there, forty were brought in. Event planners figured that that would be enough to handle four thousand teenage girls, if even *that* many showed up. And why should there be that kind of crowd? Plantation was a pretty small city.

Even before the mall opened, girls were waiting outside, milling around the parking lot. As soon as the doors were unlocked, people began to gather in the center court of the mall. Executives there were pleased and still confident they could deal with anything.

As the minutes ticked by, more and more people showed up. Long before Luke arrived, there were four thousand teens waiting, then five thousand, then six thousand.

The mall staff started to get a little anxious. There were already two thousand people more than there had been at the other mall, and Luke wasn't due to arrive for some time yet!

They couldn't call the thing off, because *then* they'd have a riot. All they could do was wait for Luke to show up and hope that things went better than they had in Washington.

More time passed. It was nearly an hour until Luke was scheduled to greet his public, and a rough count put the size of the crowd at seven thousand fans . . . then eight thousand . . . then nine thousand.

It was nearly time for Luke to appear. Word spread through the mass of teenaged humanity that the star's limousine had arrived. The girls were giggling with nervousness, standing on tiptoes to see over the heads of others, looking toward the stage where their idol would soon be standing *in the flesh!*

You could feel the excitement in the air. There were now *ten* thousand people waiting to see Luke. The floor of the mall was actually shaking and wobbling from the weight of the crowd!

Worse, there were people outside the mall, pressed against the glass doors, unable to squeeze in. Security people were concerned that some of them might actually be pushed *through* the doors.

Someone came out on the stage and a scream passed over the crowd: at first, everyone thought it was Luke.

False alarm. It was only a spokesperson. But the crowd knew, now, that Luke was about to step on-stage.

No one heard what the emcee said into the microphone, because they were all too busy screaming, "Luke, Luke, Luke!"

Suddenly, ear-splitting shrieks passed over the crowd from front to back like a wave as the gangly hero walked out on-stage, smiling that devilish smile and waving to his fans.

The crowd started to shift and move forward, like a solid mass. People started to scream, but now the shouts weren't for Luke: kids were being crushed up front as the mob surged ahead.

Fearing that the stage was about to be stormed and that more kids would be hurt (not to mention the object of their affection), representatives of the mall and of the Fox network made the quick, difficult decision to get Luke out of there *pronto*, which they did.

The mob suddenly stopped moving, and the cries quickly died down. People were stunned by what had happened and by Luke's disappearance—but there wasn't time to dwell on it.

The security people had moved in, separating the crowd into small, manageable sections and trying to get to those who had been injured.

After a few minutes, the fans were dispersing and ambulances began arriving. A total of twenty-one people had been injured, thirteen of them seriously enough to be sent to area hospitals.

As police Sergeant Joseph Bush said of the event, "The scene could be compared to the hysteria people felt for the Beatles."

Not bad company to be keeping, but Luke couldn't even enjoy the fact—not then. He'd been as surprised as the crowd when he was hustled away, and upon learning the reason, and discovering that people had been hurt, he was moved to tears.

He said gravely, "I had no idea so many people would come. I wish things had turned out differently.

"No one should have to go to a hospital because of seeing some geek from television!" Luke says. And though he's obviously far, far from being a geek, Luke's distress is typical of how precious all of his fans are to him.

After the crowd had thinned, the security agents deemed it safe for Luke to leave, and he was taken from the mall and returned to L.A., where he personally telephoned everyone who had been hurt. He also, reluctantly, canceled two more visits to malls.

It was a tragic event, but the tragedy was not only for the fans—it was for Luke as well. On the ride back to the airport, he realized he'd no longer be able to go out and meet the people, his fans, and that was something that upset him terribly.

Despite what Jason said about still being able to go out shopping and hit the movie theaters, it became obvious that, at least for Luke, those days were at an end.

Chapter 34

It's clear from the ratings and public infatuation for its stars that *Beverly Hills, 90210* doesn't have to worry about surviving anymore.

Ratings continued to climb through the summer, and by the time fall arrived the show was dancing around in the upper reaches of the top twenty. Considering that there's still twenty percent of the country that doesn't get the Fox programs *at all*, that's an amazing statistic!

Commenting on the success of the show, Ian sums it up in a very articulate nutshell.

"I think the producers were very smart to keep the comedy balanced with the drama," he says, "yet not let the show slip into being another MTV imitation."

He feels that quick cutting and loud music "would have just alienated adults," and that would have been disastrous because "we have adult viewers, too, and I think our show is a great forum for families with teenagers to recognize and become sensitive to each other's needs and fears."

But there's a downside to that kind of fame and responsibility as well.

James Eckhouse (whom you meet briefly on the set, along with Carol Potter) says that there's a danger in being *too* popular.

"When you have a lot of hype around a show, it puts a lot of pressure on." That, he says, can cause tension on the set . . . even to a cast as tight as this one.

Shannen agrees that there are dangers to their growing popularity.

"You can't all of a sudden think you can go out and do anything you want because you're a little bit famous," she says.

And how do Luke and Jason feel?

For Luke's part, he doesn't want his own popularity to affect the way the stories are written. He remembers how, back in the 1970s, on the series *Happy Days*, the rebellious, greaser-type Fonzie character started getting popular—and all of a sudden, the writers began featuring him in the stories more and more.

That intense weekly exposure cost the character some of his mystery, some of his allure . . . and that, ultimately, hurt the show. Luke doesn't want that to happen to Dylan McKay and *Beverly Hills, 90210*.

Jason, too, is worried about being overexposed week after week. He says that that's one reason he'll never complain when the other characters are featured more than he is in several episodes: *Beverly Hills, 90210*, is an *ensemble* show, and it can only work if the spotlight remains spread over everyone, more or less equally, instead of on him or on Luke.

With all of these concerns, just what *are* the producers and writers planning for future episodes of *Beverly Hills, 90210*?

How do you top some of the incredible shows they've done, which include such memorable events as:

—Dylan and Brenda making love (Brenda, for the first time).

—Brenda waiting for the results of her home pregnancy test.

—Brandon dating a senior with a baby.

—Brenda and Kelly dealing with the terrible fact that Kelly's mom is a cocaine addict.

—Steve learning that he was adopted.

136

—Brandon and Steve having to be "Home Alone" as they sit for a friend's baby all day.

—And Brenda and her mother struggling to deal with the awful wait for the results of the young girl's breast biopsy (this, less than two years after Cindy lost her beloved sister to breast cancer).

Apart from making Brandon a little less perfect, as Jason has discussed, Charles Rosin says that this fall's shows will deal with topics such as teenage pregnancy, homosexuality, Brandon becoming the object of a *Fatal Attraction*–like sexual obsession, and race relations—the result of a black family moving into the neighborhood.

There will be a mugging, which will call attention to the problem of crime.

Something will occur which will strain Brenda's relationship with her parents.

No new continuing characters will be added, but the so-called "secondary" characters (Steve, Kelly, and the others) will have a lot more to do. For example, Donna's going to learn the hard way that money is not the solution to *every* problem, while Steve's going to be brought down a few pegs when *he* tries to use cash and his ingratiating smile to get out of a scrape.

For their part, both Carol Potter and James Eckhouse are hoping there will be more of what they jokingly refer to as "fortysomething" plots—stories that will involve them a bit more.

Carol jokes that what she'd *really* love to do is shake up her perfect mom image: she says, "I'd love to do a show where the kids come home from school, the house is a wreck, and I'm still in bed."

Everyone in front of the camera and behind it hopes one thing will *definitely* happen: that just once, just *one* night, they'll beat *Cheers*!

Two things, however, will not change. Creator and supervising producer Star says that on his series, "the dysfunctional family" will remain "the norm." He says that that's important, since viewers need to feel that there are other kids out there who have problems at home. "They like to see something that says, 'I'm not alone.'"

Something else that will not change—at least, not immediately—is the teens' age: for this season, the writers plan on keeping them juniors. Stories involving senioritis, college applications, and even college itself will be saved for the years to come.

Naturally, the show will remain hot for the foreseeable future, but what about six or seven years from now? What lies in the future for these great young stars?

Jason has told us he wants to direct, but he also is busy reading scripts. There will be no first-run shows *next* summer, so when the show takes a siesta in March—leaving the cast free until August—Jason wants to make a serious move into feature films. (Which means you can expect to see the first big Priestley movie in theaters sometime around Christmas of '92.)

Luke is also planning to make a move into films, in movies that will get more exposure than the two he's made.

Except for Tori, who has written a screenplay and wants to write some more, the other stars have no definite plans other than to continue working as hard as they can on the show.

Which means that we can all look forward to many, many more hours spent with Jason, Luke and some of the most interesting people on TV.

People who are real . . . people who are a lot like us . . . our friends in *90210*.

Epilogue

The day is over.

The crew is packing up, and the actors have gone back to their dressing rooms. After taking off their Beverly Hills clothes and slipping into their jeans (except for Luke, who was already wearing 'em), they'll head for their cars and drive off, into the big, beautiful Southern California sunset.

You wait outside the big warehouse, saying good-bye to each of the actors as they emerge from inside, and thanking them for their hospitality. You hold out a script from the episode (an extra you found, one that you were able to take with you), and all of them sign the cover.

When Luke finally comes out, he's bouncing a basketball as he walks slowly from the warehouse. (He tells you that the cast plays a little hoops now and then to relieve the tension. Who's best? you ask. He says that Ian is, hands down . . . though Jason's a heckuva scrappy player.)

You feel a little like Dorothy in *The Wizard of Oz* as you stand inches from Luke and tell your personal "Scarecrow" that you think you're going to miss him the most of all—with the possible exception of Jason.

He's touched, and after signing the script, he thanks you from the bottom of his big heart for coming, before climbing into his four-wheeler and driving off.

Now everyone's gone but Jason, and you edge a little closer to where his dressing room is. You stand there, waiting.

You're sad that the day is about to come to an end, but you also know you'll cherish the memories of your visit (and your keepsake script) for as long as you live.

You're also anxious, though. Your stomach is churning because you *still* want to get an answer from Mr. Priestley—the lowdown on what body part he'd like to change!

Finally, you get your chance. Jason bounds out of the warehouse, wearing his shades, a white shirt, and tannish shorts, a backpack slung over one shoulder. He waves as you hustle over.

You soften him up by telling him that you forgot to congratulate him for being named one of *People* magazine's "Fifty most beautiful people in the world for 1991."

He thanks you sincerely, but half-jokes that the only place to go from there is to become the magazine's sexiest man alive, after which he runs the risk of vanishing into oblivion!

You assure him that that won't happen, and he wonders how accurate the magazine could be, since *he* was included but Luke and the others weren't!

Frankly, you say, some of Jason's fans who saw the issue picked it up and immediately muttered to themselves, "You mean, there are forty-nine *others?*"

He laughs at that, and then you hand him your script to sign. As he's doing that, you take a step back.

"Jason," you say, "do you remember what we were talking about this morning? The first question I asked you?"

"Uh-uh," he says without looking up as he signs his name.

You swallow hard. "I must say, you never gave me an answer."

"No?"

"No," you say. "So tell me—which part of your body do you wish you could change?"

140

There's a thick silence as he finishes with the script. You wonder if you've crossed the line, if you've gotten *too* familiar with him . . . if you're *ever* going to get an answer.

He hands you your script and peeks over the tops of his sunglasses, those incredible eyes looking straight into yours.

"You want to know what I'd change?" he asks.

You nod vigorously.

He says, "My eyes."

You're stunned. Literally shocked and bowled over. *His eyes?* Why—they're *gorgeous*, you say.

He makes a face. "Yeah, but I read they're green in one article, read they're blue in another, read they're blue-green in another. You know what? I'm not even sure what they are *myself* anymore!"

He pushes the glasses back up with a finger, grins broadly, and heads to his Alfa Romeo.

You just stand there for a few minutes, not quite believing what you've just heard. And it isn't until Jason's driven off that it hits you:

He was kidding.

For the entire day, joker Jason has been stringing you along to zing you at the last minute with an obvious hunk o' baloney!

You laugh, then you smile as you walk toward the parking lot, amazed that being the brunt of a joke could feel so darn good!

But what amazes you even more is that Jason felt comfortable enough with you to pull it.

And you hope that, in telling people about your day on the set, you'll be able to get across to fans of Jason and Luke that these two aren't just superstars, aren't just incredibly talented actors.

They're also two of the greatest human beings you've ever met!

141

Also in Fantail

THE YEAR I WAS BORN 1980
and
THE YEAR I WAS BORN 1985
compiled by Sally Tagholm

These colourfully illustrated books will enable you to discover all about the year of your birth and what makes it unique.

The books are like diaries, and whichever you choose, it gives a day-by-day picture of your year, with items of information ranging from national events to pieces of idle gossip, from the momentous to the humorous.

Packed full of exciting, interesting and sometimes bizarre news items, this wonderful series of books brings each special year to life.

Also available:

THE YEAR I WAS BORN 1981

THE YEAR I WAS BORN 1982

THE YEAR I WAS BORN 1983

THE YEAR I WAS BORN 1984

FANTAIL

Also in Fantail

WOOF! THE TALE GETS LONGER
by Andrew Norriss

More wonderful adventures about Eric the schoolboy who becomes
Eric the dog. When Eric, the boy, meets a new friend Rachel, both
end up on a hair-raising and hilarious adventure.

Find out how Eric is captured as a stray by the RSPCA, stars in a
television commercial, helps Rachel in buying a new bike for the
cycling championships, becomes a street entertainer and discovers
there are other dogs like him!

Here is another book about the adventures of Eric which will make
you laugh, make you growl...or make you want to run away with
your tail between your legs!

In the same series:

WOOF! THE TALE WAGS ON

Also in Fantail

YOUNG INDIANA JONES AND THE PRINCESS OF PERIL
by Les Martin

Aboard the Paris-St Petersburg Express as it races through the night, Young Indiana Jones helps a boy to evade the secret police.

So begins another adventure for Indy – but his new-found friend soon realizes the authorities are not so easily thrown off the track. Pre-Revolution Russia is a very dangerous place, especially for those who dare to speak out against the Czar...

When Indy steps in, the might of the Russian Empire is thrown against him, and even he begins to wonder if there is any way out of this one.

YOUNG INDIANA JONES AND THE CRUSADER'S CROWN
by Les Martin

On the trail of a medieval manuscript in the South of France, Young Indiana Jones finds himself drawn into the dangerous streets of the Marseille underworld.

But Indy has somebody to 'help' him - his least favourite travelling companion in the entire world, Thornton N. Thornton. Together they unravel the mystery of the manuscript, to discover they are not the only people with an interest in its message.

They soon become involved in a sinister conspiracy that could lead to a new reign of terror throughout the whole of France...

FANTAIL